THE DEFINITIVE GUIDE TO PLAYING COLLEGE SPORTS

WAYNE MAZZONI
NCAA Coach and Recruiting Expert

PUBLISHER

Mazz Marketing, Inc.

Wayne Mazzoni
287 Courtland Ave.
Black Rock, CT 06605

Phone: 203-260-4932
Fax: 866-209-1305

Email: wayne@waynemazzoni.com
Web: WayneMazzoni.com

ACKNOWLEDGMENTS
We would like to thank all of the college coaches, high school coaches, pro scouts, guidance counselors, and college admissions officers who have contributed information for this guide. Excerpts from *US News & World Report* articles and NCAA, NAIA, and NJCAA literature are also incorporated.

Every effort has been made to make this guide as accurate as possible. Nevertheless, you should still contact the appropriate organizations since rules and requirements change frequently. College Bound Sports cannot assume responsibility for any errors contained herein.

WE WANT TO HEAR FROM YOU!
Please e-mail any additions, corrections, ideas, or personal stories you feel would improve this guide to wayne@waynemazzoni.com

2 WHAT COACHES ARE SAYING ABOUT THIS GUIDE

"…An extremely valuable tool for high school baseball athletes. I strongly recommend it to any athlete who aspires to play college sports."
Chip Baker, Director of Baseball Operations, Florida State University

"The recruiting process can be confusing and clouded by misconceptions. This guide is very informative and a realistic tool for guiding a prospect in the right direction…a quality resource!"
Scot Thomas, Head Softball Coach, Virginia Tech University

"This Guide can be extremely valuable if it gets into the right hands. High school athletes should definitely take advantage of what it offers."
Dan Ireland, Head Cross Country Coach, Yale University (CT)

"The more information an athlete has, the more equipped he or she will be to make a better choice for college. [This book] fits that category."
Matt Centrowitz, Head Track and Field Coach, American University (DC)

"Deciding where to compete, learn and live for four years is a difficult decision. A guide like this is a perfect investment for someone in need of direction."
Ben DeLuca, Assistant Lacrosse Coach, Cornell University (NY)

"The recruiting process can be one of the most enjoyable experiences in life and yet it can be one of the most painful. This guide will give both athlete and parent a better feeling of doing the right thing when it comes to starting the process and its eventual conclusion."
Lance Harter, Head Women's Track Coach, University of Arkansas

"This guide gives you the opportunity to choose the correct school to fit all your needs, so when your athletic career is over, you are well prepared to lead a productive life."
Raphael Cerrato, Baseball Recruiting Coordinator, Brown University (RI)

"…A must-buy for any aspiring college athlete."
Bill Edwards, Head Softball Coach, Hofstra University (NY)

"…A great tool for high school student-athletes and their parents. There is a lot of critical information given with an emphasis on academic considerations."
Ken Browning, Assistant Football Coach, University of North Carolina

ADVISORS

We would like to thank the following people in the sports community for contributing valuable information to the guide and supporting our effort to help high school athletes navigate the college recruiting maze.

Organization	Advisor	Current or Former Title
ABILENE CHRISTIAN UNIVERSITY	Jon Murray	Head Coach
AMERICAN UNIVERSITY (DC)	Matt Centrowitz	Head Coach
BASEBALL FACTORY (MD)	Steve Sclafani	CEO
BOSTON COLLEGE	John Mortimer	Assistant Coach
BOSTON UNIVERSITY (MA)	Amy Hayes	Head Coach
BROCAW BLAZERS CROSS COUNTRY CAMP (VT)	John Ramsey	Director
BROWN UNIVERSITY (RI)	Raphael Cerrato	Assistant Coach
BRYANT COLLEGE (RI)	Amy Bartlett	Assistant Coach
CALIFORNIA STATE UNIVERSITY	Cregg Weinmann	Head Coach
CALVIN COLLEGE (MI)	Gary West	Assistant Coach
CINCINNATI REDS (KY)	Jim Grief	Pro Scout
COAST TO COAST ATHLETICS (OH)	Kevin Ritter	Executive Director
COCOA EXPO SPORTS CENTER (FL)	Jeff Biddle	Director of Athletics
COLLEGE OF CHARLESTON (SC)	Gregg Mucerino	Assistant Coach
COLLEGE OF NEW JERSEY	Dean Glus	Assistant Coach
CORNELL UNIVERSITY (NY)	Lou Deusing	Head Coach
CORNELL UNIVERSITY (NY)	Ben DeLuca	Assistant Coach
CORNELL UNIVERSITY (NY)	Dick Blood	Head Coach
DECKER SPORTS USA (NE)	Thomas Decker	President
ELMHURST COLLEGE (IL)	Clark Jones	Head Coach
ELON COLLEGE (NC)	Mike Kennedy	Head Coach
FLORIDA ATLANTIC UNIVERSITY	Bob Deutschman	Assistant Coach
FLORIDA STATE UNIVERSITY	Chip Baker	Assistant Coach
FOCUSED BASEBALL (FL)	Tom Hansen	President
FROZEN ROPES TRAINING CENTER (NY)	Tony Abbatine	President
HIGH PERFORMANCE DISTANCE ACADEMY (OH)	James DeMarco	Director
HIGH SCHOOL SPORTS NETWORK (PA)	Adam Stanco	Producer & Host
HOFSTRA UNIVERSITY (NY)	Mike Reid	Assistant Coach
HOFSTRA UNIVERSITY (NY)	Bill Edwards	Head Coach
HOFSTRA UNIVERSITY (NY)	Larissa Smith	Assistant Coach
HOPE COLLEGE (MI)	Stu Fritz	Head Coach
JOE ESPINOSA BASEBALL SCHOOL (CT)	Joe Espinosa	President
KEENE STATE COLLEGE (PA)	Peter Thomas	Head Coach
LEMOYNE COLLEGE (PA)	Joe Hannah	Head Coach
LONG ISLAND UNIVERSITY (NY)	Roy Kartmann	Head Coach
LOUISIANA STATE UNIVERSITY	Bob Smith	Assistant Coach
MIAMI UNIVERSITY (OH)	Bill Consiglio	Assistant Coach
MICKEY OWEN BASEBALL SCHOOL (MO)	Ken Rizzo	Director
MIKE EPSTEIN HITTING (CA)	Mike Epstein	MLB athlete
MORRIS BROWN COLLEGE (GA)	Marqus Johnson	Assistant Coach
MUHLENBERG COLLEGE (PA)	Ruth Gibbs	Head Coach

4

NEDCO SPORTS (AL)	Nick Dixon	President
NORTHERN ILLINOIS UNIVERSITY (IL)	Donna Martin	Head Coach
NOTRE DAME UNIVERSITY (IN)	Tim Connelly	Head Coach
PADUCAH COMMUNITY COLLEGE (KY)	Rick Tippin	Head Coach
PENSACOLA JUNIOR COLLEGE (FL)	Bill Hamilton	Head Coach
PERKIOMEN SCHOOL (PA)	Kendall Baker	AD & Head Coach
PRESBYTERIAN UNIVERSITY (SC)	Jeremy Farber	Assistant Coach
PUERTO RICO BASEBALL ACADEMY	Edwin Correa	MLB athlete
SACRED HEART UNIVERSITY (CT)	Seth Kaplan	Assistant Coach
SAGINAW VALLEY STATE UNIVERSITY (MI)	Fred Neering	Head Coach
SAINT PETER'S COLLEGE (NJ)	Tom Besser	Former Head Coach
SAN JACINTO COLLEGE (TX)	Rob Penders	Assistant Coach
SHIPPENSBURG UNIVERSITY (PA)	Steve Spence	Head Coach
SOUTH GEORGIA COLLEGE	Zach Walker	Assistant Coach
SOUTHERN ILLINOIS UNIVERSITY	Dan Callahan	Head Coach
SOUTHWEST HIGH SCHOOL (FL)	Javier Perez	Head Coach
SPRINGFIELD COLLEGE (IL)	Steve Torricelli	Head Coach/AD
ST. JOHN'S UNIVERSITY (NY)	Dermon Athlete	Assistant Coach
ST. THOMAS UNIVERSITY (FL)	Manny Mantrana	Head Coach
STANFORD UNIVERSITY (CA)	Dean Stotz	Assoc. Head Coach
STANFORD UNIVERSITY (CA)	Lonni Alameda	Assoc. Head Coach
SYRACUSE UNIVERSITY (NY)	Mary J. Firnbach	Head Coach
TENNESSEE TECH UNIVERSITY	Pat Portugal	Assistant Coach
TEXAS A & M UNIVERSITY	Jorge Hernandez	Assistant Coach
TODAYS MVP.COM (NJ)	Lou Santangelo	CEO
UNITED SOCCER ACADEMY (FL)	Bill Fisher	President
UNITED STATES MILITARY ACADEMY (NY)	Michelle Gerdes	Assistant Coach
UNIVERSITY OF ALABAMA	Bobby Pierce	Head Coach
UNIVERSITY OF ARKANSAS	Lance Harter	Head Coach
UNIVERSITY OF CONNECTICUT	Jim Penders	Assistant Coach
UNIVERSITY OF EVANSVILLE (IL)	Al Lopez	Assistant Coach
UNIVERSITY OF NEBRASKA	Ron Wolforth	Assistant Coach
UNIVERSITY OF NORTHERN COLORADO	Terry Hensley	Head Coach
UNIVERSITY OF SOUTH FLORIDA	Bryan Peters	Assistant Coach
UNIVERSITY OF SOUTHERN MISSISSIPPI	Clay Smith	Assistant Coach
VANDERBILT UNIVERSITY (TN)	Derek Johnson	Assistant Coach
VILLANOVA UNIVERSITY (PA)	M. O'Sullivan	Head Coach
VIRGINIA TECH UNIVERSITY (VA)	Scot Thomas	Head Coach
WEST CHESTER UNIVERSITY (PA)	Chris Calciano	Head Coach
YALE UNIVERSITY (CT)	Dan Ireland	Head Coach

Table of Contents

© 2009 Mazz Marketing, Inc. | 203 260 4932 | wayne@waynemazzoni.com | WayneMazzoni.com

INTRODUCTION

By reading this Guide, you are giving yourself an enormous advantage over your competitors—thousands of other high school athletes your age who also want to play college sports. Gaining admission to the college of your choice can be an overwhelming experience for the average high school student. The task is even more intricate for athletes.

Success requires a solid plan, attention to detail, and disciplined execution. Unfortunately, many high school athletes looking to continue competing in college do not have a true understanding of how the recruiting process works, and never reach their athletic or academic potential.

Because athletic programs often change—some coaches leave, new ones arrive—school and athletic programs change their focus and adapt to rule changes—it is important to have the most current information available in your search for the school that meets your athletic and academic needs. This Guide provides a road map for you to follow when making the jump from high school to college sports. If you avoid the mistakes most high school athletes make, promote yourself aggressively, and improve your athletic and academic skills, we are confident you will find a school that is right for you!

What We Want To Accomplish
Our goal is to help you find a college where you will be able to:

- Receive a quality education to prepare you for life after college, whether or not it includes athletics.
- Compete on a college team as a starter or an important role player.
- Possibly earn an athletic and/or academic scholarship.
- Obtain the best financial aid package to lower the expenses of college for you and your family.
- Feel confident in your college selection, reducing the chance of transferring or dropping out.

A Big Decision
We hope you're excited about the opportunity that awaits you: the chance to attend college and continue your sports career. College promises to be one of the most enjoyable, rewarding, and memorable times of your life. We want to make sure you select a school that meets all of your needs.

Choosing which school to attend is a big decision. College is where you will develop many of your lifelong friends. It can determine where you eventually live, what livelihood you choose after athletics, and the possibility of making a professional team. It's even where you may meet your future spouse.

So, devote whatever time and energy you need from now until the end of your senior year to make sure you promote yourself in an intelligent and informative way. Although your parents, coaches, and teachers can help, your future rests in your hands. Are you motivated and determined enough to do the required work? We hope so, because the results of your efforts could pay dividends the rest of your life.

Start Early
Don't wait until your junior or senior year to begin your college search. As you will learn in this Guide, finding the right school for you requires a continuous effort over an extended period of time. We recommend you begin your search once you enter high school. If you are currently a junior or senior, your effort will need to be more disciplined, intense, and focused than most other college bound athletes.

Think of the process as a job search. If you were looking for employment, would you wait for companies to call you? Of course not! You'd be proactive and let companies know that you want to be hired. That's what you need to do here.

Maintain a Positive Attitude

Unfortunately, the college recruiting process can be filled with disappointments: you don't perform well in a big game, meet or showcase; you don't have the statistics you hoped for; you learn that your top school doesn't need an athlete like you; or no one offers you a scholarship. Whatever roadblocks you face, do your best not to get discouraged. Try to maintain a positive and upbeat attitude and have confidence that you will ultimately reach your goal. Confidence is an important key to success in life, not just on the athletic field.

Assumptions

If you are reading this Guide, we assume you would like to gain a better understanding of the college recruiting process. You probably feel confused and are unsure what steps you should take to attract the attention of college recruiters. Most of your anxiety can be avoided if you are aware of the recruiting process. That's where we can help.

This Guide is loaded with useful information to give you the confidence and skills you need to market yourself and give you a better chance to identify and attend the school of your dreams.

We're also assuming that few coaches outside of your local area know your name, even if you're an outstanding athlete with tons of potential. Also, athletes from warm-weather climates, competing in outdoor sports, have the advantage of training year-round, generally making them more experienced athletes.

The opposite is true for a sport like ice hockey, where a cold climate is definitely advantageous! Although you may be at a disadvantage because of where you live geographically, don't be discouraged. We're going to show you how to generate attention from coaches all around the country, whether you live in sunny San Diego, California or chilly Bangor, Maine.

Get Your Degree

There are countless stories of high school athletes who seek lucrative professional contracts but never get them. We want you to realize you have a much better chance of becoming a successful businessperson, doctor or lawyer, if you graduate from college first. Once you receive a college degree, no one can ever take it away from you. It can help lead the way to financial security for the rest of your life.

This guide is written for high school athletes who want to compete at the collegiate level and receive a college degree. It is not written for blue chip athletes who receive national publicity, genuine interest from top schools, and invitations to the country's top tournaments or events.

Let Others Help You

It is important that you share this Guide and advice with your parents, coaches, guidance counselors, and any other people assisting you with your college search. You will benefit immensely from the opinions and experiences of people who have your best interests at heart and have been down this road before.

Why We Wrote This Guide

Since 1991, our company has helped thousands of young athletes with dreams of competing on the collegiate level. Even though most of these top athletes aspired to compete at the college level, few of them got the chance and their careers ended prematurely. We couldn't understand why this was happening so we decided to learn everything we could about the college recruiting process and share it all with you.

The information we've compiled features extensive research with hundreds of college coaches, guidance counselors, high school athletes, and parents.

Here's What We've Concluded:

The main reason so many talented student-athletes never realize their dreams of competing in college is because:

- They don't understand the recruiting process.
- They don't apply to appropriate schools.
- They don't prepare academically and athletically.
- They don't promote themselves properly.

We don't want this to happen to you!

With thousands of college athletic programs in the United States, we know there is a school out there that needs an athlete just like you.

Now, let's go find it!

CHAPTER 1

MASTER THE RECRUITING PROCESS

In This Chapter

- How college coaches recruit
- Where they go to find their athletes
- A college coach's "A-list"
- The kinds of background checks coaches do
- How a coach expresses interest in a recruit
- Some basic facts about scholarships
- Pitfalls to avoid in the recruiting process

This chapter covers the basic and not-so-basic information about the recruiting process. By the end of this chapter, you should have a better understanding of how it all works.

HOW A COLLEGE COACH THINKS ABOUT RECRUITING

You will have an enormous advantage over your competition if you are familiar with the recruiting process from a college coach's standpoint. Not every coach recruits exactly as described here—coaches at smaller schools have less money to recruit and may travel less than their Division I counterpart—but the information below is typical of most athletic programs.

A Coach Is Always Looking For Top Athletes

Coaches constantly keep their ears and eyes open for athletes who can help their teams. Naturally, they will spend the majority of their time focusing on their current recruiting class. However, if you are a talented underclassman and you impressed a college coach, either at a camp, a game, a meet, or from a newspaper article, he will probably keep your name in his recruiting database and follow your development.

"I want team oriented athletes with the ability to make decisions quickly on the field. I look for speed, quickness and toughness. I use a lot of video in my decisions and I certainly like to see each athlete in person when possible."
—Ben DeLuca, Cornell University, Assistant Lacrosse Coach, NCAA D-I

Coaches Help Each Other Recruit

College coaches belong to a small fraternity. Many are good friends, work the same summer camps, and socialize at annual conventions. Also, 30% of coaches change jobs annually and devote a lot of time maintaining their professional network of contacts. On occasion, they even share information about top athletes and assist each other with recruiting (assuming they are not rivals in the same conference).

Few college coaches can recruit every outstanding athlete they want. If a desirable athlete's grades don't meet the school's requirements, or the athlete plays a specific position and the team is already stocked at that position, the coach may recommend the athlete to other coaches in his network.

That's why it's important to develop relationships with as many coaches as you can. If you really hit it off with some college camp coaches, make an effort to stay in touch with them via mail or e-mail. Update them on your development. Even if they don't coach at schools that interest you, they could be your ticket to a college scholarship somewhere else. Remember, it's not who you know, but who knows you!

"I have a circle of other college coaches who share knowledge about different athletes. I also try to attend high school and summer league games and use scouting services. It's tough to get to them all, so we like to work off each other and help each other out."
— Jim Brady, University of Missouri-St. Louis, Head Baseball Coach, NCAA D-II

Developing an "A-list"

When the recruiting process begins each year, coaching staffs assemble an "A-list" of high school juniors they are interested in recruiting. The names on this list are athletes the coaches have seen in action at a camp, state and national meets, or tournaments. They also come from referrals by trusted sources like other college coaches, boosters, former athletes, sports reporters, pro scouts, credible recruiting services, high school coaches and even friends. Many junior college coaches also keep an eye out for "late developing" seniors.

It is important to remember that their "A-lists" are composed of high school juniors-to-be, meaning they appeared on their radar long before their junior year. With this in mind, place yourself in position to be noticed and/or evaluated by recruiters before your junior year.

This can be accomplished by playing for prominent teams outside of school, participating in college camps held by the schools you are interested in, attending showcase camps college coaches attend, and, personally notifying the coach of your interest in his program and letting him know your qualifications.

Every college team has a website, and most will have an online questionnaire. Before your sophomore year, compile a broad list of schools you would most like to attend. Take your time to list all of your athletic accomplishments, in the classroom, job experiences, and any extracurricular activities you are involved in (student government, voluntary community service).

Be proud of yourself, there is no need to be modest, but NEVER lie! Double check all the information you enter, especially your contact information. If you think your e-mail address may be inappropriate in any way (partyanimal232@yahoo.com, sexygirl37@gmail.com), create an acceptable one with a subtle indication of yourself (CHSlacrosse2@aol.com or longjumper17@hotmail.com). This can be done for free at hotmail.com, gmail.com, yahoo.com, and others.

Coaches want athletes who are willing to take the extra step. Be proactive in your communication!

Determining Who Is Interested

Questionnaires are sent to every athlete on a coach's "A-list," as well as to any athlete who writes or phones the coach's office expressing interest in the program. If you receive a questionnaire, you will be asked to provide detailed academic and athletic information about yourself and to return the form promptly. If you neglect to return it quickly, be aware that you are sending a strong message that you are not interested in being recruited. Some elite athletes on the "A-list" who do not return their questionnaires may receive a follow-up phone call to determine their interest level, but most will not. If you filled out an online version and are sent another, use the opportunity to update the coach on your latest accomplishments.

Complete the questionnaire within 24 hours. Returning it promptly does more than tell the coach you are interested in his program. It also tells him you are conscientious, able to follow instructions, and pay attention to detail. Coaches will notice if you have done your research and are organized. If you have poor hand writing, type the answers. The coach will likely notice your extra effort. Sometimes, little things like that can make all the difference in the world. While you may not stand out from the crowd by doing this, you'll definitely stand out if your questionnaire comes in late, is completed in a sloppy fashion or lacks important information.

Working With Admissions Officers to Narrow Down the List

Coaches meet periodically with their college's admissions liaison to discuss prospective recruits. This is where your athletic ability can help you get admitted to a good academic school you might not qualify for on grades or test scores alone. A coach will compile a list of his top recruits so the liaison knows which athletes are the coach's highest priorities.

Based on your academic credentials, the liaison will often tell the coach who has a chance to be admitted and who does not. Some admission departments will be flexible and accept top recruits who may fall slightly below the academic requirements, but this happens only if you are in high demand by the coaching staff.
The coaching staff will then begin to reduce their "A-list" to a more manageable and realistic pool of candidates. It will only contain students who can contribute athletically, fill a position need on the team, and possess the academic marks to get accepted to the school.

In-Home Visits

If a head coach or assistant coach comes to your house, he will want to meet with you, your parents, and maybe your high school coach. The coach's goal is to explain the benefits of his school's academic program and team, discuss scholarships and financial aid, and determine your interest level in his school. Obviously, he also wants to get to know you as a person and make sure he is making a wise investment of his time, coaching resources, and, possibly, scholarship funds.

NCAA Clearinghouse

A NCAA member coach will require confirmation from the Clearinghouse that you are academically eligible to compete in college sports. If you have not achieved the required grades, test scores, and taken the right courses, the coach will immediately eliminate you from his recruiting list. Don't get knocked out of the recruiting game before it even starts by under achieving in class. See Chapter 7 for more information on the Clearinghouse.

Core Courses

The NCAA requires a certain number of college preparatory (core) courses to be completed in high school before an athlete is eligible to play during freshman year. This requirement varies between divisions.

Make sure in your freshman year you know the current requirement for your graduating class and are taking enough core courses to qualify. If you have insufficient core courses when you graduate, you cannot compete during freshman year of college, and cannot receive an athletic scholarship. This can put a serious damper on your game. It is difficult to step away for a season and then return to peak playing condition, physically and mentally.

Athletes who fail to complete the required number of core courses will be allowed to play beginning with their sophomore year and also to receive a scholarship, but the sad truth is that a year of inactivity may cost them a valuable scholarship or starting position on the team. If this does happen, you will need to dedicate yourself to staying in shape and improving your skills.

It is imperative that you make sure at the start of your freshman year that you have planned your academic schedule to include enough core courses and that you do so each year until you graduate. It's also best to try and complete core courses as early as possible in the event that you fail required course. You'll want to have enough time left in your high school career to make it up.

Coaches Do Their Homework, Too

Before a coach decides to offer you a scholarship, he will do an extensive background check to find out everything he can about you. A scholarship is a big financial risk for the coach and his college, so coaches can be very thorough in their research, in order to improve the chances of making an intelligent decision. A few phone calls to your high school coach, guidance counselor, teachers, summer team coach, friends, and any local contacts he has will provide the information he needs.

So ask yourself right now:

- Is there anything I am doing now that will negatively affect a college coach's opinion of me? (tardiness, detention, suspensions)
- Do I attend and participate in all of my classes?
- Do I get along with my teammates?
- Am I a leader or a follower?
- What kind of crowd do I hang out with?
- How is my work ethic, drive, and integrity?

Scholarships & Walk-Ons

Once the athletic staff has finalized its recruiting list, it's time to decide which incoming freshmen or transfer students will receive athletic scholarships and how much money each person will receive. All other athletes on their recruiting list will be invited to make the team as walk-ons, assuming they still want to attend the school. Though, there is a difference between having been in contact with the coach (being recruited), and truly just walking-on after getting into the school. Those who have been recruited are much more likely to make the team and see playing time.

Telephone Calls

College coaches are not allowed to call you until July 1 before the start of your senior year. You are permitted to call a college coach as often as you like, but do not abuse this privilege and acquire the dreaded "nuisance" tag. Try to limit calls to at least every 10 days unless something important comes up. After July 1, a coach is limited to one outgoing phone call to you per week, except during these situations:

- Within 5 days before your official campus visit.
- On the day of a coach's off-campus visit with you.
- On the initial date for signing the National Letter of Intent and two days after that.

Also note that text-messaging communication between a college coach and a recruit is not permitted, regardless of degree of interest.

Letter of Intent

At the NCAA D-I level, there is an early signing period and a late signing period where a coach will try to persuade his top recruits who have been offered athletic scholarships to sign a National Letter of Intent. This letter is a binding contract that guarantees the recruit will enroll at their school. Even if you plan on signing a Letter of Intent, still send out back-up school applications, just in case.

NCAA D-I and D-II schools must wait until September 1 of your junior year before sending you promotional items like school or team publications, media guides, and schedules. Begin a filing system for what you receive, so when a coach e-mails, you will have information about the school readily available. Make note of all games these schools play in your area and go to as many as possible. Also, review these materials before you visit the school.

Facts About Scholarships

The number of full scholarships that each school can distribute is strictly limited. Each coach decides how to award his scholarship allotment. It makes the most sense to divide the allotment into several partial scholarships as opposed to giving only a few athletes full scholarships. It's a lower risk strategy because some of the scholarship recipients will fall short of expectations, get injured, become academically ineligible, or drop out.

Also, realize that the scholarships are not just earmarked for incoming freshmen, but are used for all athletes on the team. This may include as many as 35 (or more!) sophomores, juniors, seniors, and fifth-year athletes. The number of scholarships also varies by sport and association—baseball and softball teams at NCAA DI schools, for instance, have 11.7 and 12 total scholarships respectively. Other sports, such as football are allowed to give as many as 85 scholarships, while a sport such as basketball or fencing will have many fewer.

The NCAA has two ways of distributing scholarships among athletes: by team headcount and by equivalency. Head count is a maximum number of athletes on a team that may receive scholarships funds during each year. These sports are men's basketball and football (limited to 25 per class), and women's basketball, tennis, volleyball and gymnastics. Equivalency sports are limited by a dollar amount per school.

While also staying under the cap, these schools must make sure the money is not distributed to more than that sports maximum allotment. A baseball coach must make sure that his scholarship spending is not only less than that permitted in dollars, but may not add up to more than 11.7 full scholarships at his institution.

The point is, there are very few sports in which a coach can offer every participant a full ride. What also may happen is that an upperclassman may have scholarship increased in an effort to retain that athlete. A quarter scholarship may be increased to a half scholarship, for instance, which means the "extra" scholarship money has to come from another athlete's allotment.

As a result, thousands of outstanding high school athletes are never offered even partial scholarships. Many don't even receive passing interest from coaches. Keep in mind that scholarship awards are on a year-to-year basis. While a coach cannot guarantee you will receive the same award in future years, it is normal practice that it will be renewed at the same level.

Even if you are fortunate enough to get all or some of your tuition paid for with an athletic scholarship, you may still have other significant costs like room and board, books, entertainment, and transportation to and from school. D-III and D-I Ivy League and Patriot League schools do not offer any athletic scholarships (American University, a Patriot League member is the exception). Military academies like Air Force, West Point, Navy, and the Coast Guard are tuition-free; however admission requires a congressional recommendation.

In addition to allocating scholarships, a coach can consult with financial aid officers on your behalf to determine what non-athletic aid might be available. However, you should personally check out other areas of help since you cannot expect the coach to explore all of your available options. If possible, contact the team's academic counselor. Most schools have a designated counselor to assist with the administration.

If you go to a state college that is not in your home state, explore living off-campus for your junior year. Then apply for in-state tuition to cut your tuition by, in most cases, 50% or more. You will likely need to provide a copy of your lease, an in-state driver's license, or a tax return from that state.

© 2009 Mazz Marketing, Inc. | 203 260 4932 | wayne@waynemazzoni.com | WayneMazzoni.com

Likely Letters

If you are offered an athletic scholarship, you must inform the college in either November or April if you are going to accept it. Since you will not hear from the admission or financial aid office until mid-April that you have been accepted to the school and offered a financial aid package, you will receive a "Likely Letter."

This states whether you are likely or unlikely to be accepted to the school and receive a financial aid package. The "Likely Letter" allows you to make an informed decision about where to go to school, without forcing you to void the scholarship.

One Athlete's Lost Opportunity
Samantha Kent, 21, Brooklyn, NY

In high school, I was a four-year track star. Unfortunately, I did not compete in college. My friends couldn't understand how an All-County sprinter could just give it up. Truth is, I didn't give it up, I just never gave myself a chance to run.

I was convinced a college coach would offer me a track scholarship. Instead of being proactive with my college search, I waited for college coaches to find me. I was sure I would be noticed.

My times were good enough to get some attention so there was no need to worry. No one told me I had to take the initiative and write letters, and attend national meets. What a mistake! Now I'm a college senior, on the verge of graduating, and I never stepped foot on the track.

I had a great time at school, but when I graduate in May, there will be an empty feeling inside of me. I should have competed. I know I could have competed. I was even friends with some of the others on the team.

It would have been a perfect fit. If I had only aggressively promoted myself in high school, I'm sure I would have had more options and a much more rewarding college experience.

12 PITFALLS TO AVOID

Most high school athletes never get the opportunity to compete after high school. It's important for you to understand the main reasons why this happens. Avoid their mistakes and you will substantially improve your chances of competing in college.

1. I Only Want To Compete For A High-Profile NCAA D-I Team.

Once you reach your search on the country's top programs, you will be disappointed. Too many high school athletes think that programs like UCLA, Florida State, Miami, Stanford, Michigan, and other high-profile schools are the only respectable ones in the country.

While many high school athletes dream of one day competing at a top NCAA Division I school, in reality, very few get the opportunity. According to our research, roughly two percent of all high school and junior college athletes who seek to compete at a D-I school will ever get the chance.

If you're just finishing your junior year of high school, you'll have a pretty good idea if you are talented enough to compete at that level. Blue chip athletes recruited by these nationally ranked schools are often:

- ◆ All-State or All-County awarded
- ◆ Receive recruiting calls and letters from numerous coaches
- ◆ Attract many college coaches at their games

If you're not a blue chipper, no worries. Here is a list of some professional athletes and the list of their alma-maters. Bet you'll never see these schools on ESPN Sports Center!

NBA Athlete	College	NFL Athlete	College	MLB Athlete	College
Ben Wallace	Virginia Union	Dominic Rhode	Midwestern State	Ben Sheets	NE Louisiana
Chris Anderson	Blinn	Jake Delhomme	Louisiana-Layette	B.J. Ryan	SW Louisiana
Darrell Armstrong	Fayetteville	Jimmy Smith	Jackson	Billy Wagner	Ferrum
Derek Fischer	Arkansas-Little Rock	Joe Horn	Itawamba	Jeff Francis	Lethbridge
Ronald Murray	Shaw	London Fletcher	John Carroll	Joe Nathan	Stony Brook
Speedy Claxton	Hofstra	Rod Smith	Missouri Southern	Mike Piazza	Miami-Dade
Steve Nash	Santa Clara	Terrell Owens	Tenn.-Chattanooga	Terrell Owens	Holmes

LESSON LEARNED: If you are not a "blue-chip" recruit, expand your college search and include a wide range of schools on your target list.

"I'd say 75% of athletes don't research schools like they should. In four years, I want them to look back and realize that they made the right decision. They have to pick the best fit for them, not the biggest name. College is expensive…you want to make sure you do the right thing."
- Amy Hayes, Boston University, Head Softball Coach, NCAA D-I

2. I Must Be A Hot Recruit. Coaches Send Me Letters All the Time.

Do not assume form letters in your mailbox mean that a coach considers you a prospect. Every high school athlete who expresses interest in a college team, regardless of his ability, will receive a letter and questionnaire in the mail asking for more information. In fact, some schools may send out as many as 10,000 letters each year!

Understand that this is only an initial request for information and, in most cases, an expected courtesy.

Answer the following questions honestly:

- ◆ Do college coaches call me?
- ◆ Is my mailbox overflowing with letters from coaches who want me to consider their schools?
- ◆ Are coaches coming to my house to meet with my parents and me?
- ◆ Do recruiters travel specifically to watch me compete?
- ◆ Have I been approached by a coach at recruiting camps, showcases, or tournaments?

If you're one of the lucky few who can answer "yes" to some of the above questions, then consider yourself a blue-chip prospect. If you're like most high school athletes, however, and you had to answer "no" to all or most of the questions, then you need to take a pro-active approach to your college search.

LESSON LEARNED: Receiving phone calls, personalized hand-written letters from college coaches, and requests for personal meetings is a much better indicator rather than form letters and questionnaires of how interested a coach is in recruiting you.

3. I'll Make the College Team as a Walk-On.

If you only receive lukewarm interest from coaches, but you really want to compete in college, you can try making the team as a "walk-on." This means you try to prove yourself to the coaching staff in the fall or preseason tryouts.

However, understand that it may be difficult to make the team as a non-recruited athlete. Your odds of success are not high because the coach has likely recruited only where the team has room. Every now and then a coach may find a "diamond in the rough," who has gone unnoticed. For the most part, however, a coach knows exactly which athletes will comprise his squad before the open tryout even begins. This is another reason why failing to match your actual skill level with the competitive skill level of the school you are trying to compete at is a mistake.

LESSON LEARNED: Even if you make the team, you may have a slim chance of ever competing. You may want to search harder for a school that wants you and that you fit with talent-wise. Many athletes who try to "walk-on," not including "recruited walk-ons" who we will discuss in Chapter 5, may quit the team and transfer or drop out after their freshman year. Check out our "Hit the Web" section in Chapter 4 for the best way to search for schools that fit your talent level.

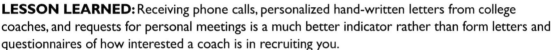
"We only have a few walk-ons each year. I urge those looking to walk-on to contact coaches and let them know you are interested in the program. Then, just work on your skills and stay in shape."
-Amy Barlett, Bryant College, Assistant Field Hockey Coach, NCAA D-II

4. My High School Coach Is Going To Get Me A Scholarship.

Do not rely on your high school coach to contact college coaches, write letters, or solicit offers on your behalf. Most high school coaches are unable or unwilling to devote the large amounts of time required to help their athletes find the right college. If your coach has time to assist you with the recruiting process and has demonstrated a commitment to help you find a school that meets your needs, consider yourself lucky.

Too frequently, we hear from parents that their child's high school coach doesn't do anything to help. Often these complaints come in the spring of a high school athlete's senior year, after most college application deadlines have already passed.

Don't worry if your coach only limits his involvement to practices and games. Some coaches, for whatever reason, do not feel college recruiting is part of their job responsibility. Some are simply too busy to help. Others are unfamiliar with the recruiting process and might not even know where to begin. Many coaches who sincerely want to help are restricted in their efforts simply because they don't have that many college contacts, except perhaps locally and at the college they themselves attended.

While thankfully rare, there occasionally exists a coach who is vindictive for one reason or another simply because of a personality conflict. Some coaches devote all of their time to the "star athlete," because he's the easiest one to promote. These are reasons you need to take the initiative and take charge of your recruiting processes. Remember what's on the line in the recruiting game is your future, not your coach's. Don't sit back and wait for someone to help you.

LESSON LEARNED: Don't expect your high school coach to devote much time and effort to assist you with your college search. Ask him to help, but take responsibility and control your own future. The college coach will be impressed by your personal accountability.

5. I'd Be Happy Just to Make the Team.

Always set high goals for yourself. We have found that athletes who have the best college experience are the ones who get the chance to compete on a regular basis. Sitting on the bench during the big game is no fun unless you have the potential to work your way into a more competitive role within a short period of time. Ask yourself: would you rather be the big fish in a small pond or a small fish in a big pond?

LESSON LEARNED: Find a team where you can contribute and have a realistic chance to compete everyday. You'll have a much more enjoyable college experience.

6. Lots Of College Coaches Will Watch My High School Games.

If more than a handful of college coaches ever watch you compete throughout your high school career, you are in a select group. Even if coaches attend your games, they most likely represent only nearby schools. Most athletic recruiting budgets do not allow coaches to travel around the country scouting talent. It's just too expensive. Coaches will scout regional high school and summer tournaments or events, usually within a couple hours of their hometown, but rarely will they travel farther. It's just not financially feasible or an efficient use of their time.

It's not unusual for a college coach to spend the majority of his travel and recruiting budget scouting a select few blue-chip prospects. What's left in the travel budget will be used to attend national events where the greatest number of prospects can be seen in one place, i.e., showcase events and regional and/or national tournaments.

Say for example you live in Minnesota and are interested in attending a college in Texas. Even if the coach in Texas really likes you, he probably won't have the money or the time to fly to Minnesota to watch you compete. He would rather find out if you are going to attend any events where he can see you and a number of other athletes on his target list. Or, he may invite you to attend one of his summer camps.

LESSON LEARNED: Be pro-active and take your skills to coaches of the schools that interest you. Don't expect them to travel to your hometown.

7. Small Colleges Have Weak Teams.

Most athletes believe the misconception that NCAA D-I is the only way to go and that all other college divisions are inferior. Don't fall into this trap! If you do, you will eliminate hundreds of great schools that may need an athlete just like you.

If the school is a very good fit academically, take time to learn about the coach and the team. You may be in a situation where a young team is on the rise or if a talented new coach has recently been hired, they might be poised for a breakout season with your help.

LESSON LEARNED: Surprisingly, many D-II, D-III, NAIA, and junior college teams stack up well against D-I schools. Don't neglect them simply because of their affiliation.

8. I'm Only Considering Schools Where I Can Earn A Full Ride.

Full-ride scholarships are extremely rare and not as readily available as most athletes and parents think. Most scholarship money is divided into partial scholarships.

LESSON LEARNED: Don't expect that an athletic scholarship will allow you to attend school for free. Even if you are one of the fortunate few to receive an athletic scholarship, you will probably still have to pay for other college expenses with family money, an academic scholarship, or loans.

9. I'm Only Applying to My First-Choice School.

Even if your heart is set on attending one particular school and the coach has expressed interest, you should still promote yourself to other schools. It will give you leverage when it comes time to discuss academic and athletic scholarships, or financial assistance, with the coach and admissions office.

The coach at your first choice school has all the bargaining power if he finds out that you are desperate to attend his school. Plus, you might find that a different school—one you might not have thought of before—is a better fit for you.

LESSON LEARNED: Leverage is crucial if you want to increase your worth and potentially attain a better scholarship. Avoid the temptation to prematurely tell a coach that you've made your decision to attend his school. Explore every option.

10. I'm Regularly Told by High School or Travel Club Coaches that I have the Ability to Compete at the Division I Level.

Constant praise from influential people is nice to hear, but it can also be dangerous. It may cause you to sit back, wait for college coaches to find you, and not be aggressive in your search. The only opinions that matter in the end are those of the college recruiters.

There's another reason that college coaches don't rely too heavily on an athlete's high school stats. It's understood that high school officials and scorekeepers often inflate an athlete's statistics.

LESSON LEARNED: Always strive to improve your skills. Never stop learning. And, as they say in the business world, don't believe your own PR!

11. If a Coach From a School Outside My Target List Wants to Recruit Me, I'll Tell Him I'm Not Interested.

Avoid rushing to judgment if a coach expresses interest in recruiting you. A lot can change in a few months. A school that you dismiss now may look a lot more attractive later on. Never lie to or mislead a coach, but you should also avoid making snap judgments. Make sure you research every opportunity before deciding.

Coaches don't waste time when it comes to recruiting. If they show interest in you, it is because they think you will have a positive impact on their program. While it may seem obvious that coaches will go after the best athletes possible, coaches try to keep their recruit list realistic. A DIII basketball coach who has finished among the middle of his conference the past couple years isn't going after the same athletes being looked at by UNC and Memphis.

Once you decide exactly where you want to go, and after you have signed a Letter of Intent, tell the other coaches who are interested in you to remove you from their recruiting list. Make sure to thank them sincerely for their interest in you. Not only does it show good character, but if you ever want to transfer, that school may still be a good option.

LESSON LEARNED: Keep your options open! Avoid rushing to judgment until you have made up your mind. You should also visit each school that shows interest in you—it's the best way to decide if it's a place you not only want to compete for, but make your new home as well.

12. Coaches Will Notice Me When I Have A Big Senior Season.

If you play a winter or spring sport, you may already know where you are going to college by the time your senior season is underway. Also, some coaches have already made up their "A-List" of recruits and narrowed it down to their top priority prospects by the fall of your senior year. Play your best every year to increase the chances of a coach noticing you earlier on.

LESSON LEARNED: Your junior year could be your most important recruiting time period.

CHAPTER 2

ENERGIZE YOUR SUPPORT GROUP

In This Chapter

- Advice for parents who want to help
- Making your guidance counselor your advocate
- Your high school coach can be your secret weapon

You are definitely not alone in the process of solving the college-recruiting puzzle. There are many people ready and willing to help you if you just ask. You need to develop your own cast of advocates, first to help you create a list of colleges best suited to you, and then to help you apply and gain admission.

This chapter helps you identify and energize the people who can improve your chances of reaching your athletic and academic goals. It also includes some information specifically designed for your parents, the people who have the most at stake financially and emotionally in how your college selection process moves forward. So, even if they can't take the time to read this Guide, at least make sure they review this chapter with you.

PARENTS

Dear Parents,

It's a challenge to strike the right balance between offering guidance to your child and taking control of the entire college search process. If your child is like most teenagers, you will need to constantly provide gentle reminders so he stays focused on the search. You've helped your child get this far, now it's time to guide him to the next level.

In this chapter we discuss some of the ways to help your child prepare for one of the biggest decisions and transitions of his or her young life. The objective: help your child get accepted to a college, receive the best education possible and have the opportunity to compete in collegiate sports — in that order.

It's A Big Country, So Think National

The United States is blessed with many wonderful things, including the best, largest, and most diverse higher education system in the world. There are dozens of colleges that would be a good academic and athletic match for any high school athlete, including yours.

The first commandment of developing a Target List of appropriate schools is to start with an open mind and a blank slate. "What's the right school for my child?" is an open-ended question with more than one right answer.

Discourage your child from fixating on a single "dream" school, unless he or she is an absolute lock to get in and is one of those unusual kids who knows exactly what they want in life. Even then, we recommend you look at other schools just in case. An important lesson to teach during this process is to ALWAYS have a back-up plan. We hope you will not learn this the hard way and will plan accordingly.

If you plan on paying for your child's education with a full-ride scholarship, you're probably in for a rude awakening. College athletic scholarships are hard to come by and rarely cover all of your child's expenses. It's great to win the lottery, but not too smart to plan on it happening.

It's Okay to Be Nervous, But Try Not To Grab The Wheel

Helping with the research and applying to college reminds you of the separation soon to come and the undeniable fact that your teenager is moving toward adulthood. This can make you nervous and emotional. You may feel tempted to take control of the evaluation and application process, particularly if your child is not being as diligent and focused as you would like. You got this far, now help your child prepare to accept the responsibility of college life, even if he or she doesn't plan on going too far away.

Your job is to support your child's decision about college. Managing this process on his or her own is a critical element in the mental and psychological preparation for leaving home. He or she can handle it and so can you!

As the process unfolds, remind your child that because he or she applied to a variety of colleges, and also worked hard at academics and athletics, acceptance to at least one school is likely. Your child will make new friends, have fun, be challenged, and get a great education. When the decision letters arrive, re-emphasize your support, and if necessary, remind your child of the fickle nature of the whole selection process.

Stay In the Background

Nothing is worse than a parent who steals the spotlight. Many parents, especially successful ones, are accustomed to manipulating the system to make it work for them. Resist the temptation. The admissions process is the time for your child to stand on his or her own. Parental attempts at influence peddling often do more harm than good.

Don't Live Vicariously

Many parents subconsciously relive their own hopes and dreams through their children. Some want their kids to follow in their footsteps; others want them to achieve things that they themselves never could. Still other parents see their children's college admission as proof they deserve an A+ in parenting. Having high hopes for your child is natural, but try to spare him or her the burden of unreasonable expectations. One of the greatest gifts you can give is the freedom and the support to follow his or her own dreams, not yours.

Communicate

Encourage your son or daughter to think through the basic questions:

- Why do you want to go to college?
- What are your most important needs and goals?
- What size school would feel most comfortable?
- Do you want to stay close to home, within driving distance or an airplane ride away?

Communicating with a teenager is not always easy, but look for the moments that present themselves, and they will. Being available to talk when your child has a question or wants to express a feeling is extremely important. This is probably the first time he or she is dealing with a decision of this magnitude, so try to be patient and give the time and space to communicate his or her's thoughts and fears.

Set Financial Parameters

Although we have been stressing up to this point that the college selection process should be managed by your child, there is one part of this picture over which you have the responsibility and the obligation to assert your control: dollars and cents.

If you're in the market for a Chevrolet, it doesn't make sense to spend a lot of time at the Mercedes dealer ogling cars you can't afford. Likewise, if your resources can't support a tuition of $30,000 per year, have that conversation with your child before starting to develop a Target List of schools. This will be a necessary and healthy dose of real life for both of you.

You and your child will be terribly disappointed if you end up falling in love with a school and a program that is simply beyond your means, and you have to say "sorry, keep looking." Go on-line and find a list of all U.S. colleges sorted by tuition expense. Chapter 8 features a list of great web sites to help you with your research. No matter what your budget, your child is sure to find plenty options

If your child is accepted to a school that is too expensive, thoroughly explore financial aid options. The school can offer advice and let you know what is realistic.

Be Realistic

Don't set your child up for failure by encouraging him or her to apply only to schools that may be out of reach. Look honestly at your child's academic record and athletic ability, and then study the admissions profiles of the colleges on the Target List. If Stanford is our of reach, don't swing by Palo Alto on your college tour. Make sure to apply to at least two colleges where your child is over-qualified and can expect to be accepted. Then, even in the worst-case scenario, if he or she isn't accepted to a first choice school, you have a viable Plan B.

Your perception of your child's athletic ability will not earn a scholarship. The college coach's opinion and other respected and objective appraisals are the only ones that matter.

Encourage Your Child to Stay On Schedule

Review the High School Checklist (see Chapter 8) with your child to make sure you stay on track and do the required work. Don't let your child procrastinate and put it off until senior year of high school. Athletes who do their research and prepare early have the most opportunities.

Support, Support, Support!

You can lighten the workload by providing books, web addresses, returning questionnaires, assisting with background research, and following the advice in this Guide. Just make sure to stay in the background, in a supportive role. If you discover a potential gem of a school, pass along the web address and let your child explore it. Share your own college decision-making memories. Convey your understanding of how intimidating the process can seem so your child can benefit from your experience.

Be a Cheerleader

Be generous with your praise for your child's accomplishments. Remind him or her that the acceptance or rejection to a particular school will not change a person's worth as an individual. The world is filled with highly accomplished people who didn't attend prestigious universities.

Encourage Your Child to Focus on Academics

The higher the grades and test scores, the more sports opportunities your child will have. Make academics a priority and do whatever is necessary to convey the importance of constant improvements. If your child is not reaching academic potential, find someone who can help, whether it's a private tutor, a teacher, or a friend. Make sure that you make this assessment by sophomore year so your child will have time to get better.

Senior year is too late to address this!

Even junior year is cutting it close. Be aware that there are some student-athletes who figure that their senior year is a time to "take it easy" and enjoy their last year of high school. This is often the time that some students' grades take a nosedive. Don't let "senioritis" happen to your child. College admissions reps frown on this. It's possible for an offer to be withdrawn in the event of a shoddy senior academic year.

"Academic" Athletic Showcases

Some specialized showcases only invite talented athletes with superior grades and SAT or ACT scores. These showcases are held for strong academic schools that are also interested in recruiting some top-flight athletes. Schools like Rice, Notre Dame, Stanford, and Northwestern fit this category. Even though the Ivy League and Patriot League don't provide athletic scholarships, they often assist the athlete with academic scholarships and grants. Besides athletic ability, athletes invited to these specialized showcases may have to meet at least one of the following academic criteria: 3.3 grade point average, 1650 SAT score, or 24 ACT score.

Discuss Majors and Potential Careers

Talk about potential majors that may interest your child. Discuss what your child would like to do for a career. He or she may not have an answer, but it's something to start thinking about. Encourage your child to seek advice from successful family friends who work in the same areas of interest. Your child may even be able to intern at a local business to gain valuable experience.

Mentoring opportunities also exist for students to be advised by someone in the field they're interested in. Students who have clear career goals, or at least have put some thought into what they want to do after sports impress coaches. It's a sign of maturity many coaches appreciate and value.

"If you don't get it done in the classroom, you can become ineligible or distract yourself from the job on the field. I look for athletes to look sharp, play hard, and maintain grades. If I don't have to worry about them in class, then I can concentrate on softball."
–Scot Thomas, Head Softball Coach, Virginia Tech University, NCAA D-I

Visit College Campuses

From the time your child enters high school, make an effort to visit as many different college campuses as you can. You can attend sporting events, concerts, go on campus tours, and participate in open houses. Let your child experience the colleges that you or other family members attended. If your family vacations, visit schools in that area. Once your child reaches junior year of high school, limit your visits to schools that he or she is seriously considering. Schedule your trips so you can watch the team compete. These unofficial visits will give your child enormous insight and help decide what kind of school to attend.

Get Periodic Updates

It is important to periodically phone or meet with your child's teachers, guidance counselor, and coach. This will keep you informed of your son or daughter's progress and allow you to confirm that he or she stays on course and meets academic requirements.

Don't Write Your Child's Application

Most colleges require essays as part of their application process. Advisors caution parents not to edit their child's essays, since admissions officers can distinguish easily between the writing of a 45-year-old and that of a 17-year-old. Instead, review the application folder for mistakes or omissions. Once it has been sent, do not call, write, or e-mail the admissions office. All communication should come from your child.

Step Aside

If your child gets rejected at a particular school, the worst thing you can do is call the school to complain and tell them they made a mistake. Admission officers are more apt to listen to a direct appeal from your child than from a disappointed parent. Also, resist the temptation to call coaches and write letters on your child's behalf. Most college coaches would rather communicate with an athlete than a parent. It demonstrates that the athlete is mature and responsible.

Split Up On College Visits

Many counselors advise parents to avoid the temptation to accompany their children everywhere on campus. You may even want to skip the guided campus tour and let your child experience it on his or her's own. Most admissions officers won't allow parents into the interview, but will entertain a few questions afterward. While you wander around campus, your child can sit in on classes, talk to professors and hang out with students.

Deal With Rejection

If the dreaded rejection letter arrives from your child's top-choice school, don't turn the disappointment into your own. With this response, your son or daughter is apt to feel like he or she have failed you, too. Let your child be upset. Be around in case he or she wants to talk about it. Explain that from your perspective, it doesn't matter where he or she goes to college. Say you are sorry and that you understand the disappointment. Leave it at that. Focus on the schools that accept your child.

One Parent's Mistake

Alyssa Williams, New Haven, CT

In high school, my son Aaron was a three-year starter on the varsity team and was voted Team MVP his senior season. He wasn't the most dominant athlete in our region, but everyone knew who he was. I figured he would have college coaches offering scholarships to him. I couldn't have been more wrong!

By the start of his junior season, I was expecting coaches to show up at his games to watch him play. Aaron expressed interest in a couple of college programs by sending introductory letters during the previous winter. He even got some responses back with questionnaires attached.

After I met with his high school coach, I was confident the coach would use his connections to help get Aaron a baseball scholarship. His coach knew a lot of people at the collegiate level and assured me everything would work out.

As his senior season approached, a lot of Aaron's friends were getting accepted to schools. I told him to go out and put up the kind of stats he was capable of and everything would fall into place. Aaron finished his senior year as a member of the All-County team with a .448 BA, 12 HR, 47 RBI and 0 scholarship offers.

They say mothers know best, but in this case, I didn't. I should have encouraged Aaron to take a more pro-active approach promoting himself to college coaches.

Luckily, his grades were good enough to get accepted to a strong academic college; yet the only competing he did was with his fraternity's intramural squad.

GUIDANCE COUNSELOR

For better or worse, guidance counselors are likely to play a crucial part in your college search and application process. They will write recommendations for you that, come April of your senior year, will help determine whether you receive fat envelopes full of enrollment materials or skinny ones with rejection letters.

A guidance counselor can monitor phone calls from admissions officers with questions about a low grade on your transcript or a discipline problem. And if you wind up getting rejected everywhere you applied, a sympathetic counselor might even plead your case to admissions officials at schools that still have open slots. These are professionals you definitely want in your corner, so don't be shy about making the first move. It's also advantageous to include someone whose primary perspective is academic.

Learn Your Way Around The Office

While your guidance counselor is getting to know you, get to know your counselor's resources. Ask for a tour of the guidance office and have the counselor recommend college guidebooks, videos, and web sites. Find out whether your high school hosts workshops on college admissions and attend every session possible.

Use Your Counselor's Connections

Your best college resource may be your counselor's connections. If your counselor visits a lot of campuses and invites many admissions officers to your school, she probably plugged into the college admissions scene. Admissions officers who know and trust your counselor may ask for the inside scoop on you. Your counselor will know which schools are most likely to accept you, which ones should be considered as "safeties" and which ones are long shots. We're stating the obvious here, but, take advantage of this professional's knowledge.

Provide Good (and Bad) Information

If your counselor is too swamped for frequent personal chats with you, drop off a resume that lists your recent accomplishments. Create a portfolio of your best papers and creative projects, and don't be shy about disclosing any family situations that may affect your academic performance. For instance, if one of your parents gets seriously ill and your grades slip as a result, tell your counselor so she can explain your situation. Once you establish a personal rapport with your counselor, e-mail may be a more acceptable way to stay in touch on routine matters.

Regular Meetings

Your counselor should meet with you and your parents at least once in your junior year and again early in your senior year. Topics can include your academic strengths and weaknesses, sports, test scores, whether you should take a prep class, and college suggestions to consider. You should also drop by the office at least once a month from your junior year through graduation.

Your counselor can confirm if you are in compliance with NCAA eligibility requirements, explore potential career opportunities, identify colleges that specialize in your area of interest, and discuss the pros and cons of each school on your Target List.

Although most counselors are conscientious and knowledgeable, occasionally they may make an honest mistake, which could cost you a scholarship.

Here's a real-life example of a high school athlete who took Spanish I in junior high (8th grade) and Spanish II and III as a freshman and sophomore in high school. His guidance counselor said that colleges would consider that as completing three years of a language. As it turned out, that was true of a state university where he lived, but wasn't for lots of out-of-state colleges, that only counted it as two years. The student failed to qualify at the school he wanted to play at, which happened to be an out-of-state school with different requirements.

Make sure you and know the academic requirements of the school(s) you'd like to attend. A good place to start is to check the NCAA Eligibility site, as well as the school's admissions office. Make a checklist of all necessary classes you'll need to get into the schools you are applying to. Use this list to make a long term schedule so you can schedule these classes as early as possible, in case you need to re-take any.

Overcoming Failure
by Tom Hanson, Ph.D. Redefine "failure."
Your personal statistics and your team's record are outside of your control. You can influence them, but not control them. Focus your energies on things you can control: your preparation, your focus, your attitude, and your commitment. If you define success as doing a great job with the things you can control, and failure as focusing on things you can't control, you'll give yourself the best chance of competing at a top level AND be a lot happier!

Focus on this moment. There's nothing you can do about the past, and nothing you can do now about the future. NOW is where the action is! The great athletes keep it simple, and one way to do that is to keep your focus consistent. If you've had a bad day, go ahead and feel bad for awhile. That's okay. But remember, your poor performance is in the PAST. Before you go to bed that night, shift your focus to what you can control NOW: getting yourself into the best possible mindset for the next game.

These ideas are simple, but not easy. Partner with a buddy, coach, or parent to help stay focused.

Tom Hanson, Ph.D., is a mental toughness coach who helps athletes, coaches and parents produce breakthrough results. Last year he worked full-time for the New York Yankees, and previously consulted with the Texas Rangers, Anaheim Angels and Minnesota Twins.

Help Developing a Plan and Timetable
Many counselors believe their job is not to tell students where to apply, but to advise them how to go about the process. Doing the legwork for students, counselors say, won't teach them the survival skills they need for college. A good counselor will direct you toward books and online resources. We will direct you to Chapter 4 where we tell you how to identify appropriate colleges for you and develop your Target List.

Use History to Help You
Generally, high schools keep lists of where previous students have and haven't been accepted. Schools with more sophisticated programs also maintain a database on the records of students who were accepted and rejected at various colleges. Counselors should analyze the data to track athletic admissions trends and use them to guide applicants. Organized feedback from high school graduates about what they like and dislike about their colleges, and about how prepared they felt academically, is also useful information for you.

Be Vigilant
If you are put on a waiting list at your first-choice college, your counselor can call the college to promote you and let the admissions department know you really want to go there. If the outlook is dim, your counselor

can provide suggestions about alternatives. If a qualified student strikes out everywhere (a high school's worst nightmare), a dedicated counselor will call around to find out which colleges have space available.

Find a Counselor Who Will Help

While it may be tempting to avoid your counselor, that's almost always a mistake. If your counselor resists all advances or simply doesn't know enough about colleges to be helpful, make an appointment with another counselor at your school. If asked, tell your assigned counselor that you are gathering additional information.

You can also consider going outside the school for college advice. But be warned that your high school counselor can't be avoided entirely. He or she will still write your recommendation, and colleges will not contact the independent advisor if they want to know more about you. Never fear, though. College admissions committees know that, for a variety of reasons, not everyone receives adequate counseling—or a fair recommendation.

Counselors-For-Hire

You could hire an educational consultant to help you develop a list of schools and prepare applications. A consultant's services usually cost from $700 to several thousand dollars (ouch!). Princeton Review and Kaplan Test Prep and Admissions also offer one-on-one counseling. Less personalized counseling is also available in seminars or online packages. If you are truly needy, you can turn to groups such as Bottom Line, which counsels students for free. Many pricey consultants also offer free counseling; so don't be afraid to ask.

Red Flags

No matter which independent counselor you hire, be sure to first check out her qualifications. Reputable counselors belong to either the Independent Educational Consultants Association (703-591-4850) or the National Association for College Admission Counseling (800-822-6285).

Ask prospective counselors for professional references and call them. A few things to avoid: inexperienced consultants who claim their Ivy League degrees give them special insight into the admission process; independent counselors who have poor relationships with guidance offices (you can't afford to alienate your high school counselor!); and consultants who promise entrance into prestigious schools before viewing your academic record. If it sounds too good to be true, it usually is.

A Guidance Counselor's Plea

Richard Douds, High School Guidance Counselor, Raleigh, NC

A lot of students come to me for academic advice, but I'm equally qualified to help them advance athletically. My high school guidance counselor played baseball for Wake Forest and knew what the recruiting process was all about. He helped me get a scholarship using his connections, and I would love to do the same for my students, no matter what sport they play. Unfortunately, they don't seek my help. It's tough for me to promote students if they haven't taken the time to come see me first.

Once I get to know my students on a personal level, it's easier to give college coaches the information they want. I enjoy helping students develop a plan to achieve their goals. Many of my colleagues don't know a lot about the recruiting process and wouldn't know what to say to a student looking to play at the collegiate level. I tell them to have their students come talk to me if they want advice. It's really no burden.

HIGH SCHOOL COACH

Take Responsibility For Your College Search

Do not depend on your high school coach to research potential schools, phone coaches on your behalf, or eventually land you a college scholarship. If your high school coach is supportive and wants to help you, consider yourself fortunate and be sure to thank him or her.

Don't worry, however, if your high school coach is not as involved as you would like and only devotes time to team practices and games. Even though you would like to believe your coach is responsible for helping you with your college search, it is not officially part of his or her's job responsibilities.

Remember, you have many teammates who would like to receive the same kind of personal interest. So, if your coach wants to help you, gratefully accept the assistance. Remember that coaches often have full-time jobs and families, so it is difficult for them to balance their obligations, just as it is for you with school and your friends.

Ask Your High School Coach to Initiate Dialogue With Coaches

After you mail your Letter of Interest and Athlete Profile to your Target List (see Chapter 5), ask your high school coach if he or she would be willing to do some or all of the following:

- ◆ Write an evaluation of you and send it to your target schools.
- ◆ Phone each coach on your Target List to confirm the school's interest in you and recommend you.
- ◆ Clarify the college's decision-making process.
- ◆ Stimulate interest if the coach is not recruiting you.

Use Other Sources for Help

Find someone who will assist you if your high school coach cannot. This person must be someone who has credibility and be familiar with your skills:

- ◆ Opposing high school coach
- ◆ College coach
- ◆ Former athlete who gives you lessons
- ◆ Summer or travel team coach
- ◆ Alumnus in your sport of one of your target schools
- ◆ Assistant Coach

A High School Coach's Conflict Coach

Mike Rivera, Baltimore MD

My students assume my day starts at 7:20 AM. In reality, my day starts well before that. My 30-minute commute north from Annapolis starts around 6:30 AM and I'm awake an hour before that. I teach math five out of eight periods and also hold advising and office hours. When I'm not in the classroom, I'm grading tests, tutoring students, and devising lesson plans. A lot of my students end their day with the last bell around 2:00 PM. At this point, I've been out of my house for nearly eight hours and my day is only beginning.

At the end of eighth period, I replace lesson plans with game plans. Aside from my duties in the classroom, I'm also the head coach in two different sports. I hold daily practices from 2:30-5:00 PM, and on game days, we're usually done around 8:00 PM.

Fifteen-hour days are tough, especially with a 1/2 hour commute tacked on each way.

A lot of my athletes ask me to help them get scholarships, and I do the best I can to assist them, but there isn't enough time in the day. I write evaluations for all my athletes and call college coaches on their behalf, but I can't help everyone. I know how stressful the recruiting and college selection process can be on my athletes and their parents, which puts me in an awkward situation.

I would love to help all of my athletes get scholarships, but it's more important for me to see my students pass math. First and foremost, I'm a teacher.

FINISH LINE: Sit down separately with your parents, coach, and counselor. Tell them about your goals and dreams for college. Ask them for help in the process, and come to an agreement about how much, and what type of help it will be. Then, make a list of all your resources and determine how you will use them to help you get recruited. While most of the time these people are very reliable, always be ready with a back up plan to handle extra responsibility.

CHAPTER 3

HOW TO IMPROVE YOUR PROFILE

In This Chapter

* Improving your approach to athletics
* Developing your leadership abilities
* Increasing your physical skills
* Improving your grades and test scores
* Staying focused in the classroom

No matter how many compliments you've received about your athletic achievements, your grades, or your personality, there are always ways you can get better.

This chapter focuses on ways to improve your profile (and no, we don't mean the side view of your face), so that you are more "recruitable" by college coaches.

© 2009 Mazz Marketing, Inc. | 203 260 4932 | wayne@waynemazzoni.com | WayneMazzoni.com

ATHLETIC SUGGESTIONS

At the risk of stating the obvious, your athletic ability is the most important factor in determining whether you will suit up in a college uniform. Never assume that you are finished learning as an athlete or that you know everything about your sport. You must constantly absorb information and strive to improve your ability.

Even professional athletes spend thousands of hours in the off-season working on the physical and mental aspects of their game, so you know there's no such thing as too much practice for a high school athlete.

Understand what's in your control to improve. Some physical characteristics like your height and body structure may not change, but there are areas within your control that you can improve:

- Strength
- Flexibility
- Endurance
- Speed
- Mental Toughness

You'll have to work extremely hard and demonstrate unyielding motivation in order to separate yourself from the thousands of other athletes who are looking to play at the college level. If you know you are weak in a particular aspect of your event do something about it...right now!

Seek Constructive Criticism

In order to improve, first identify which areas of your athletic performance needs work. It's always nice to hear praise from your parents and receive backslaps from your teammates, but a little constructive criticism from the experts is even better. Consult an experienced high school coach, college coach, or professional athlete who has seen you compete. He will be able tell you the exact areas to improve and recommend specific drills.

Seek as many opinions as you can. Ask your coach to be completely honest about your weaknesses. You may not agree with his evaluation, but you can use it as a starting point for your development. It is also important to respect your coach's opinion and consider the advice. In addition to learning where your game could improve, make sure you set aside the time for drills to convert your weaknesses into strengths. This will not only help you in the long run, but have instant game-changing effects.

If you have mechanical flaws, fix them immediately to avoid making them a permanent part of your technique. Videotaping yourself in a practice setting is an excellent way for you to recognize exactly what you are doing wrong and it's a great way to solicit feedback from others who haven't seen you compete in person.

Take Your Game To The Coaches

Exposure is key to the recruiting process. The more coaches who see you perform, the better chance you have to generate interest. Don't wait for coaches to come to you. Be pro-active and take your game to them. Your goal should be to generate as much national interest as you can, so you will have a wide array of options when it comes time to sign a National Letter of Intent. If you live in New York and want to compete in North Carolina, you better make sure southern coaches see you compete in person.

"As a high school lacrosse athlete from Massachusetts, I had my eyes set on several Mid-Atlantic schools. To make sure I was noticed by coaches in the region, I would often travel to tournaments, showcases, and recruiting camps in the Pennsylvania, Maryland and Delaware. I was able to meet with lots of head coaches at a top recruiting camp held at U. of Maryland. Long story short, I just finished a great career at my number one choice."
–Rob Hickey, Widener University

It is unusual for a coach to offer a scholarship to an athlete no one on his staff has seen compete. It's too much of a risk. That's why you need to find out how you can compete in front of the coaches on your Target List. This will also give you a reality check of how you measure up against other athletes with similar goals.

Call each school and ask the coach what tournaments or showcases the staff is attending. Also, ask to be put on their mailing list and notified when off-season camps are conducted, and any other pertinent information. Just make sure the coaches on your Target List see you in action.

Stay In Shape

It is extremely important to stay in shape year-round. Again, take your cue from the pros who work hard in the off-season to stay fit. Whether you decide to concentrate on one sport, or participate in multiple ones, is your decision. However, do not become inactive at any time and don't stray away from your training.

Staying in top physical form demonstrates to college coaches that you are serious about your commitment to your sport and your future. Also, it's good for your health and will improve your academic effectiveness.

Become A Leader

Coaches admire athletes who demonstrate a winning attitude, mental toughness, take charge of workouts, and composure under pressure. These traits will not only make you a better athlete, but they will help you elevate the ability of your teammates as well. So, be a leader, not a follower.

If you're not one of those "verbal types," lead by example with your work ethic in practice and your desire to improve. If you are one of those athletes who likes to talk to your teammates, keep it positive and enthusiastic. Whatever your personality, strive to be someone who is described by his coach and teammates as a "student of the game," "great team mate," and a "winner."

"I look for athletes with positive attitudes who always hustle. In addition, they must have an inner drive to accomplish things both as an individual and on a team level. A leader makes those around him better and shows a commitment to doing things right the first time."
–Dan Ireland, Head Track Coach, Yale University, NCAA D-I

One coach discovers the "leaders" at tryouts by asking who wants to lead a drill. The athletes who jump out and lead the warm-ups, for instance, have just shown they are leaders.

Don't be negative! An athlete who openly criticizes teammates for errors is not the kind of leader coaches want. On the other hand, the athlete who openly and sincerely boosts a teammate's confidence after a miscue is exactly the kind of leader coaches love and recruit for their squads.

While not everyone is a natural leader, be sure to demonstrate your dedication and discipline at all times. You are held to higher standards as a student-athlete. More people will pay attention to your actions than other students, whether it is on the field, in the classroom, in social settings, and the library and cafeteria.

Use this to your advantage and as a reason to always do your best, stay focused, and set a good example to others.

How Many of These Leadership Qualities Do You Possess?

- ◆ Have a strong desire to win and always do your best.
- ◆ Seek tough competition.
- ◆ Welcome a difficult task.
- ◆ Set high, but achievable goals.
- ◆ Be willing to admit mistakes and accept constructive criticism.
- ◆ Practice on your own; go beyond what your coach asks of you.
- ◆ Enjoy the responsibility that accompanies leadership.
- ◆ Be willing to work harder than anyone else, especially when the coach is not watching.
- ◆ Possess confidence in your ability.
- ◆ Focus and concentrate on the task at hand.
- ◆ Learn from your mistakes and try not to repeat them.
- ◆ Maintain composure.
- ◆ Don't get easily discouraged or frustrated by errors, mistakes, or poor officiating.
- ◆ Understand the importance of continuous coaching.
- ◆ Respect your parents, coaches, officials, teammates, and opponents.
- ◆ Put the team's needs before your personal needs.
- ◆ Get along with your teammates; offer support when they have a problem.
- ◆ Understand that championships are won in the pre-season.
- ◆ Watch your language and avoid profanity.
- ◆ Encourage your teammates and do not belittle your opponents.
- ◆ Maintain a positive appearance and good body language.

WHAT MOTIVATES A WINNER...
Coach Rob Kelso, University of Houston

- ◆ A winner displays characteristics that set him apart from all others.
- ◆ A winner always wants to be the best that he can be.
- ◆ A winner is never satisfied with his performance. He is committed to preparing and open to change, and always wants to succeed, whether it's a high GPA or a better athletic performance.
- ◆ A winner learns from his failures and he never makes excuses.
- ◆ A winner always looks for ways to improve his performance and to add value to the team.
- ◆ A winner always expects to be victorious.
- ◆ A winner is not afraid of risk.

Attend Prospect Camps at Your Top Target Schools
Most college coaches run their own camps for high school athletes. These weeklong camps are packed with instruction, guest speakers, and informal competition.

Attending camp is an ideal opportunity to gain exposure with the assistant coaches (the ones who do the bulk of the recruiting), get a feel for what these coaches like, and visit the campus. From the coach's standpoint, he is getting to know you as a person and an athlete, evaluating not only your talent but whether you would be a good fit in his program.

ACADEMIC SUGGESTIONS

Before a college coach decides to recruit you, he looks at your GPA, core courses, and SAT/ACT scores to make sure you meet his school's admission standards. If you are way below the minimum requirements, he will not waste his time recruiting you, regardless of how much you could help his team. Poor grades assure you of only one thing when it comes to college admissions and sports: fewer choices.

If you are the fastest runner, the best shooter, or throw farther than anyone in your state, junior college will be your only option if you are not strong enough academically to be admitted to a four-year school. Even an All-American caliber athlete with a poor academic record will give a scholarship-equipped coach pause.

Coaches know that athletes who don't perform in class are more likely to become academically ineligible or flunk out at the college level. And that may be more risk than a coach is willing to take. If a coach has only one scholarship left and he must choose between two athletes of equal talent, he will always select the better student.

Improve Your Grades and More Schools Will Recruit You

Say for example you have a 2.6 GPA and 1000 SAT score. While those marks are average, you've automatically taken yourself off the recruiting lists of probably 500 strong academic schools! Imagine how many more opportunities you will have if you meet the admission requirements of all schools in the country, or at least a higher percentage of them?

I place very high expectations on academics. That's what you're here for. You go to college to grow as a person and learn some of life's skills. I expect maximum effort in the classroom. Sports will compliment that."
—Marcus O'Sullivan, Head Track Coach, Villanova University, NCAA D-I

Schools have very different requirements, and you need to be aware of them. For instance, in California, getting into the top state-sponsored universities (University of California system) requires very good grades as well as very specific requirements for high school classes. A biology class you took in your high school in Nebraska may not have the content they require.

Other schools in other states often have similar "extra" requirements. Check out each school you're interested in to make sure the high school classes you take will qualify. There have been instances of a students who have graduated from high school with good grades, met all the Clearinghouse requirements and still were unable to meet the college entrance requirements.

While this isn't the norm, it still happens often enough that you need to be prepared. Identify as early as possible the schools you're interested in and make sure they don't have "above and beyond" requirements so you still have time to do something about. Make a check list of every class and requirement that must be met for you to get into each of your target schools. Do not think of these classes as an extra burden; make the best out of them to learn as much as possible to prepare yourself for college classes.

Set high goals for yourself in each class you take. Do not settle for mediocrity. Be disciplined with your homework and strive to reach your full potential. If you're receiving B's right now, go for A's. Ask your teacher for extra help, hire a tutor, form a study group with your friends, or take a preparatory SAT/ACT course. Take Advanced Placement (AP) classes if you can qualify for them.

Do whatever it takes to improve your academic standing and do not believe for one second that grades are unimportant. Nothing impresses a college coach more than athletes who work just as hard in the classroom as they do on the playing field.

Adopt the "10% rule." It is simple. Just do 10% extra in everything you do. Whatever your coach, your teacher, your parents, or your employer asks of you, go above what is required. Try it. You'll be amazed at the results.

Be aware of the classes in high school that are seen as "Easy A's". Avoid these at all costs because they are the result of a teacher that doesn't care or a curriculum that is below your intelligence. While it is always good to have an "A" on your report card, consider this a gift. Make sure you truly earn the A by doing extra reading and studying. To truly become a well-rounded college athlete, you need as much knowledge as possible.

Also, always be the first to arrive at the game or practice and the last to leave. This will allow you to take extra time to care for your equipment, meet with the trainer, and get mentally focused. "Gym rats" are highly prized commodities!

Manage Your Time Effectively

Since your daily schedule is already filled with classes, sports, and extracurricular activities, it's important you set aside a block of time each night for homework and your college search. Make it a priority and be disciplined. You will reap the rewards for many years to come.

A great tool is a weekly or monthly planner you can hang on your wall. This will allow you to set time aside for your top priorities. If you are able to stick to a schedule where you set aside specific time for homework, your college search, training and exercising, and "you time," you will easily transition to the even busier college life.

Develop Other Interests And Get Involved In Extracurricular Activities

College admission officers look favorably on students who have multiple interests and are involved in a wide range of activities. Find an organization at your school (i.e. school newspaper, peer counseling, Safe Rides, Drama Club, Band, Foreign Language Club, etc.) that interests you and get involved. Also, you may want to volunteer a few hours each month at a local charity or non-profit organization.

More than one school will take an applicant with a 3.5 GPA who's been involved in extracurricular activities and community service, over an applicant with a 4.0 who's done nothing else. A mother in California told us her son was the class valedictorian, yet was turned down by UCLA and Cal because he didn't have any extracurricular activities.

Recently, a counselor urged one student, a TV-sports addict, to get off the couch and get involved. The student started writing a sports column for the high school paper, coaching basketball in a poor neighborhood, and interning at a local television station. The counselor is betting that he'll have several admissions offers to choose from next year.

Don't worry about trying to become a "Renaissance Man or Woman" at age 17. Not many high school seniors are the perfect, well-rounded student. Just show a passion for one or two of your strongest interests. Do not simply build a resume that lists every club in your school. What impresses admission officers is proof that an activity is a theme in your life. Think quality, not quantity.

Work To Increase Your GPA

If you did not perform well in your freshman year of high school, you may be given the benefit of the doubt if your grades go up in your sophomore, junior, and senior years. Your goal should be to graduate ranked as high as possible in your class. And, by all means, avoid "senioritis." Don't think that you can coast as soon as your applications are finished. Colleges will notice if you drop an AP course, take an easy schedule, or let your GPA slide in your senior year. Some schools will even pull admission offers from a student who performs poorly in his senior year.

Hire A Tutor or Enroll In A SAT/ACT Preparation Course

Ask your guidance counselor for suggestions to raise your college entrance exam scores. Kaplan and Princeton Review offer outstanding courses you may want to consider. Taking a prep course will boost your confidence tremendously. Some students hire private tutors or purchase online study programs.

You will most likely need to take these exams several times until you are satisfied with your scores. Where the SAT's use your top combined score, it is best to thoroughly prepare for everything your first time through. This way you will be able to use your experience to see exactly what will be asked, so you can use your following attempts to concentrate on specific areas.

Regardless of which exams you take, don't assume a higher-than-average score will guarantee acceptance to your dream school. Test scores are not weighted as heavily as most people think they are; although, poor scores can be difficult to overcome. It's just another part of the admissions package.

Take Advanced Placement or College-Level Courses

College admission officers will view you as a motivated student if your high school transcript features honors and AP courses. Your GPA may slide a little, but it's worth it to take advanced classes in areas where you are strong.

For example, if you've always received good grades in math, take AP calculus and AP statistics. If writing and reading are your strong points, take AP English. Remember, your transcript is the most important piece of your application. Many admission officers would rather see you challenge yourself than get straight A's in easy courses. Many colleges "weight" AP classes by scoring them half a grade higher than "regular" courses for the student's GPA.

Spend Your Summers Productively

Admissions deans don't look kindly on summers spent relaxing at the beach, but otherwise they're surprisingly open-minded. If you need money, take that fast-food restaurant job, and then try to make the experience as meaningful as you can. You might sign up for a community college course or summer enrichment program, for example, or do volunteer work. Also, since your an athlete, you may be able to find work at a local sports camp. This may even help you network with college coaches on staff.

Take Both Entrance Exams

Virtually all colleges accept both the SAT and ACT, so you may want to take them both and just feature the better score on your application. To determine which you'll find easier, take a practice version of each and compare your scores using a concordance table (www.collegeboard.com has one available online).

FINISH LINE: You've just learned about some of the ways you can improve your profile as you get ready to be a part of the recruiting process. Using the list below, make a note about where you rate in each of these areas, and where you'd like to be.

	Excellent	Average	Needs Work	Goal
Athletic	❑	❑	❑	_____
Leadership	❑	❑	❑	_____
Endurance	❑	❑	❑	_____
Foot Speed	❑	❑	❑	_____
Strength	❑	❑	❑	_____
Flexibility	❑	❑	❑	_____
Attitude	❑	❑	❑	_____
Practice Habits	❑	❑	❑	_____
Relationship w/ coach	❑	❑	❑	_____
Relationship w/ team	❑	❑	❑	_____
Non-Athletic	❑	❑	❑	_____
Grades	❑	❑	❑	_____
SAT/ACT Scores	❑	❑	❑	_____
Time Management	❑	❑	❑	_____
Work Ethic	❑	❑	❑	_____
Attitude	❑	❑	❑	_____

CHAPTER 4

YOUR COLLEGE LINEUP

In This Chapter

* How to rank schools by academic factors
* Making sure you will like the campus life
* Reasons to target certain schools
* What to look for in the athletic program
* How to cross-reference your athletic and academic needs and desires

In order to become the focus of college coaches on the hunt for new athletes, you've got to work hard to make them aware of who you are and what you can do. This chapter is about another step in the recruiting process: Doing the research and investigation required to create a Target List of schools that meet your academic and athletic needs.

From your Target List, there will be 7-12 schools you will apply to and one that you may ultimately attend. Coaches from these schools will hear from you, evaluate you at their camps and showcases, and hopefully your high school coach and guidance counselor will reach out to them as well. Ironically, at the beginning of this process, it's you who will be doing the recruiting of the college coach you want to compete for.

CREATING YOUR TARGET LIST

STEP 1: Who Are You?
Let's start by trying to identify the schools that interest you for academic and personal growth reasons. Why start with academics? Because chances are, like 99.9% of all other college bound high school athletes, you may not have the good fortune of earning a living as a professional athlete.

> If you want a great online resource for college searching, *US News & World Report* (www.usnews.com/) offers a fabulous search engine that you should definitely explore.

At the end of your college career, you will leave campus with at least three priceless assets: great memories of college sports, friends you will have for life, and a diploma. After you've thrown your last pitch, run your last race, or scored your last goal, your degree, and the education it represents will be your ticket into the career of your choice and the beginning of your adult life.

The best way to begin evaluating schools is to first evaluate oneself. Once you know your own strengths and weaknesses academically, personally and athletically, it will be much easier to match yourself with different colleges. Describe yourself according to these categories:

- Academic likes and dislikes: Which subjects do you enjoy the most? Math (Calculus, Trigonometry, Physics, etc), English, History, Psychology, Sociology, Economics/Business, Science (Biology, Chemistry, etc.), Art (Landscape Painting, Movies, Sculpture, etc)
- Extracurricular: Which recreational activities (after school athletic program, peer counseling, Boy or Girl Scouts) community services (volunteer at local soup kitchen, or tutoring program) and religious activities (participate on regular schedule?) do you currently participate in and hope to continue in college?
- Personality Traits: Are you shy or outgoing? Independent or prefer a structured environment? Want to be far from home or within driving distance? Hang out with different kinds of people?

"What's the best college for me?" is a multiple-choice question with more than one right answer. What we are trying to help you to do is divide the enormous melting pot of American colleges into manageable servings, creating boundary lines between broad categories of schools. As long as you focus on schools that feel right for you, a good choice will be made no matter which school you ultimately select.

Say, for example, you want a medium-sized school with a suburban campus, within driving distance from home, a strong business faculty and a competitive Division II team. There may be up to a dozen schools which fit this criteria, and the differences among them will be much less significant than say, the difference between a big state university and any school in your target group.

Once you have written down as much information about yourself as possible, it's time to begin looking at schools and learning about which ones look promising and which ones you can eliminate from consideration. Below are the factors that work best to quickly screen colleges and enable you to develop a small but reasonably diverse list of schools which you can then visit or research in greater depth.

Factor 1: Location, Location, Location
Just like in real estate, location is an important consideration when trying to whittle down a list of colleges from hundreds to dozens. Schools are either "nearby," "within driving distance," or "a plane ride away." The

closer to home you wish to be, the more schools you can cross off your consideration list. Conversely, if you have no preference about being far away, then location is less of an issue for you.

Work with your parents on this one because where you go to school obviously has a big effect on how often you will see your family over the next four years. There's also a cost element to consider as getting to and from school can be thousands of dollars a year for flights, rather than the cost of a tank of gas.

Likewise, do you want to be in a rural, suburban or urban setting? On the walk from your dorm to the library, will you encounter shattered glass and boarded-up houses, or ivy-clad brick buildings and broad expanses of green?

During your downtime, will you go snowboarding or snorkeling, apple picking or clothes shopping? Many students also underestimate how strongly the weather can affect their spirits and ability to succeed. If you live in a warm southern climate, love the beach and have never seen it snow, make sure you understand that going to college in places like New York, Boston or Chicago will require a rather significant lifestyle adjustment.

Local companies tend to actively recruit on campuses, leading many graduates to settle in the area where they attended college. So quite often, your choice of a college impacts the region you settle in for good, not just for four years.

Factor 2 - Size Matters

The size of a school—how many students and square miles of campus—is also very influential on the quality of your college experience. Big schools with tens of thousands of students are like medium-sized cities unto themselves. Do you want to walk to class or take a shuttle bus? Be able to meet in person with your professors after class? Choose from hundreds of clubs and organizations to join (for example, there are 900 clubs and organizations at the University of Wisconsin-Madison)?

The advantages of a big school are many—incredible academic and extracurricular choices, lots of different people from different places to meet, and well-financed athletic teams and facilities.

Depending on your personality, however, you may find these pluses don't outweigh your concerns about large class sizes, the impersonal nature of such a big community, and having to interact with the bureaucracy which manages today's modern universities.

Smaller schools, on the other hand, typically have smaller classes, a more intimate social environment, and a generally more accessible administration. Combine your size and location preferences and you probably have made a great start toward narrowing the list of schools you research further.

Factor 3 - Majors Are Minor Issues, For Now

What do you want to major in? It may be the most popular question asked to college bound high schoolers as they enter application season. While it's fine, perhaps even an advantage, to know what you want to major in at college, it's also perfectly okay to be undecided. So why bring it up here? Well, if you're one of those young people who know exactly what she wants to study—engineering, hotel management, or agricultural science, for example—you certainly will have an easier time creating a list of colleges to focus on.

Your major will not necessarily dictate where your career will take you. A recent History major grad from Gettysburg College is now a Regional Sales Manager for a sports marketing company.

If you're the opposite type and have no idea what you want to major in, then you probably would want to avoid the specialty schools which means you too can narrow your list. For students in between, who can't specify what they do or don't want to study, no worries. Most students arrive at school with one major in mind and then decide to switch, sometimes as late as their junior year of college. If you aren't sure what direction to take, just concentrate on schools with lots of options. Most schools even require undeclared students to take a class that will help with self assessment towards a desired major. It's okay to be flexible in life and in college majors

Factor 4 - Campus Culture
You will do your best academically if you feel like you fit in on campus. Reflect on your social life in high school. Are you looking for a school that offers more diversity? Less? Do you want to spend your nights at film festivals, frat parties or studying?

During campus visits, take time to observe students and see how they interact with each other. Talk to students on campus and ask how people with different backgrounds and interests get along. College is an amazing place where you will grow emotionally and intellectually.

You will have fantastic new experiences in class, with friends and in athletics. Only you know which kind of environment suits you best. So be honest with yourself and try to steer toward settings that match up with your comfort zone while still holding out the promise of exciting challenges and opportunities.

Factor 5 - Social and Academic Freedom
Do you want to go to a college where students are treated like adults, make their own decisions about where to live, which classes to take, and are graded on just midterm and final exams? Tired of following rules and schedules set by parents and guidance counselors, many college-bound high schoolers would answer with an emphatic "Yes!"

Well, be careful because it's a tricky question. Sudden immersion into a life with few rules isn't always easy. For one thing, if you have freedom, so does everybody else—including the kids who are carousing outside your door the night before your chemistry midterm.

Are you the kind of person who is easily influenced by your friends? If the honest answer is yes, then a school with too few rules or a big school where it's easy to get lost in the shuffle may be the wrong place for you. It's probably better to explore schools where classes are evaluated on a more consistent basis to help you stay on track.

Colleges differ widely on the matter of how much freedom they grant undergrads. Some schools have lots of detailed rules, like class attendance requirements, designated residential facilities, and restrictions on parties; while others are very hands-off except for extreme behavior such as plagiarism, cheating, or threats to others. Remember, no school is going to babysit you. No matter which school you choose, you are going to have more freedom than you ever had living at home.

Having thought about whether you would blossom or flounder in an unstructured environment is an important element in the college selection process. Remember, whichever path you choose, you will meet up with hundreds or thousands of young adults who felt the same as you. It would be a shame to arrive at school as a freshman and suddenly discover that you hadn't considered this particular issue carefully enough and were out of sync with your new classmates.

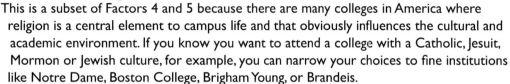

Factor 6 - Religion

This is a subset of Factors 4 and 5 because there are many colleges in America where religion is a central element to campus life and that obviously influences the cultural and academic environment. If you know you want to attend a college with a Catholic, Jesuit, Mormon or Jewish culture, for example, you can narrow your choices to fine institutions like Notre Dame, Boston College, Brigham Young, or Brandeis.

If you want the kind of structural, social, and cultural trappings that come with an academic institution that identifies with a particular religion, you are fortunate enough to live in a country where these choices are both available and plentiful. Just do your homework on the schools you are looking at so you know what to expect.

Factor 7 - Diversity

Many colleges, particularly private ones, make a concerted effort to attract minority students in increasing numbers. If you're going to be a modern success, you must be capable of understanding and dealing with individuals whose backgrounds are different from yours. It will also make you a better human being.

Guidance counselors caution students to look at more than statistics when considering diversity. They suggest you consider whether the curriculum embraces other traditions and whether residence halls tend to be integrated or segregated. For schools where the commitment to diversity is made in earnest, the opportunity for you to acquire a deeper understanding of others can be a large reward.

Factor 8 - Academic Qualifications

If you are a C student with a lower SAT score, there are many schools you will not qualify for academically, so just scratch them from your list and move on. Not everyone can go to an Ivy League school and not every Ivy League graduate is a success in the adult world. Our point is simple and obvious: be optimistic, but also be realistic.

Take into account the minimum academic performance each school is looking for before you put it on your Target List. This is one of those cold realities of the college selection process. While its fine to have a couple of schools on your Target List that would be considered as "stretches," make sure you also end up with schools where you are well within the range of their academic requirements.

We've listed eight factors that we believe can help you quickly and effectively narrow a huge pool of schools to a Target List of a dozen or so colleges; a group small enough for you to research each institution individually and put them in order of preference. We have provided you access to a directory of all college coaches and other very useful resources for this exact reason.

Next is Step 2 where you'll need to evaluate athletics to see which of the schools on your Target List also suit your athletic needs.

HOW SOME SCHOOLS STACK UP

Aside from choosing a school to compete at, you are also choosing a new home. It is important that you are comfortable with all aspects of life on campus. Here are how some schools stack up, in no particular order, according to Kaplan's book, *The Unofficial, Biased, Insider's Guide to the 320 Most Interesting Colleges.*

Best Value
Rice U., TX
U. of Kansas, KS
U. of Minnesota, MN
Oklahoma State U., OK
U. of Nebraska, NE
U. of Wisconsin, WI
Texas Tech U., TX
U. of Maryland, MD
Berea C., KY
Penn State U., PA
U. of Virginia, VA
C. of New Jersey, NJ
U. of Arizona, AZ
U. of Michigan, MI
Yale U., CT
West Virginia U., WV
Purdue U., IN
U. of California, CA
U. of Notre Dame, IN
Rutgers U., NJ
U. of Washington, WA
Harvard U., MA
U. of Colorado, CO
U. of Missouri, MO
Truman State U., MO
Virginia Poly & State U., VA
U. of Texas, TX
Duke U., NC
U. of North Carolina, NC
Miami U., OH
Washington U., MO
James Madison U., VA
Cornell U., NY
Stanford U., CA
U. of Delaware, DE
Texas A & M U., TX
Tulane U. LA
Grove City C., PA

Best Academic Facilities
Brown University, RI
Georgetown University, DC
Mass. Inst. Tech., MA
Kenyon College, OF
Pomona College, CA
Columbia University, NY
Lafayette College, PA
Claremont McKenna College, CA
Cooper Union, NY
Bowdoin College, ME
Davidson College, NC
Illinois Wesleyan University, IL
Amherst College, MA
Haverford College, PA
Bucknell University, PA
Emory University, GA
Northwestern University, IL
Cornell University, NY
Colgate University, NY
Cal. Institute of Technology, CA
Carleton College, MN
Bates College, ME
Colby College, ME
Middlebury College, VT
Princeton University, NJ
Dartmouth College, NH
Rice University, TX
Grinnell College, IA
Harvard University, PA
Johns Hopkins University, MD
Duke University, NC
Stanford University, CA
Swarthmore College, PA
The Colorado College, CO
University of Notre Dame, IN
University of Pennsylvania, PA
University of Richmond, VA
Vassar College, NY
Washington and Lee University, VA
Washington University, MO
Webb Institute, NY
Wellesley College, MA
Wesleyan University, CT
Williams College, MA
Yale University, CT

Best Freshman Housing
U. of California, CA
Texas A & M U., TX
Kent State, OH
U. of Texas, TX
Rice U., TX
U. of California, CA
Stephan F. Austin State U., TX
Illinois Wesleyan U., IL
Miami U., FL
Penn State U., PA
Stanford U., CA
Indiana U. of Penn, PA
U. of Central Florida, FL
Florida State U., FL
U. of Utah, UT
Michigan State, MI
Texas Tech U., TX
Wright State, OH
U. of Illinois-Urbana, IL
New York U., NY
Ball State U., IN
Grand Valley State U., MI
Marshall U., WV
Oklahoma State U., OK
Stonehill C., MA
U. of North Carolina, NC
Washington State U., WA

Best Party Schools
Bloomsberg U. of Penn., PA
California State U., CA
East Carolina U., NC
Florida State U., FL
Penn State U., PA
San Jose State U., CA
Southern Illinois U., IL
Southwest Texas State U., TX
SUNY at Albany, NY
U. of Texas, TX
U. of Florida, FL
U. of Georgia, GA
U. of Massachusetts
U. of Miami, MI
U. of Missouri, MO
U. of Virginia, VA
U. of Wisconsin, WI
Washington State U., WA

Hot & Trendy
New York U., NY
Arizona State U., AZ
U. of California, CA
George Washington U., DC
Pepperdine U., CA
Boston C., MA
Florida State U., FL
Brown U., RI
Stanford U., CA
Duke U., NC
Boston U., MA
San Diego State U., CA
Harvard U., MA
Mass Inst. of Tech., MA
U. of California, CA
Texas A & M U., TX
Penn State U., PA
U. of Arizona, AZ
Princeton U., NJ
Georgetown U., DC
U. of Colorado, CO
U. of North Carolina, NC
U. of Maryland, MD
U. of So. California, CA
U. of Florida, FL
U. of Texas-Austin, TX
U. of Miami, FL
U. of Virginia, VA
U. of Wisconsin, WI
Virginia Poly Inst., VA
Wash. U. Saint Louis, MO

STEP 2 - Will I Contribute?

Step 2 is to take your Target List and research each school's athletic program. Place them in order based on whether you think you have an opportunity to make the team and contribute. At the top of this list would be schools where you feel you could step right in and compete your freshman year. At the bottom of the list would be the schools where you're not sure you would even make the team.

Make sure that you visit www.collegecoachesonline.com every few months and search for schools that meet your criteria. This is an extremely valuable resource that you definitely want to use. A free one-year subscription is included with this guide. Email info@collegeboundsports if you misplaced your login password.

Focus On Schools Where You Can Contribute Athletically

We think it's worth repeating: the most important athletic factor to consider in prioritizing your Target List is the likelihood of competing. Since it could be unlikely you will play pro, what's the point of spending your last four years in the sport you love sitting on the bench?

Be Prepared To Play In Any Division

It's a good idea to include schools from every division (NCAA, NAIA, and NJCAA) on your Target List. Don't get hung up on Division I schools. There are schools at every level that can meet your athletic and education needs.

Honestly Assess Your Athletic Ability

- ♦ How have you performed at showcases, tournaments, meets, State Championships?
- ♦ Do you know any college athletes with abilities similar to yours?
- ♦ Do you possess impressive physical attributes? A coach may recruit you if he believes that you can develop into a great athlete over the next 2-3 years.
- ♦ Do you possess the leadership ability necessary to compete in college?
- ♦ Do you play for competitive summer or club leagues?
- ♦ Would you benefit from playing for a year or two at the junior college level, or even a post-graduate high school?

Keep in mind that you may compare yourself to the other athletes on your team, in your league, or ones you compete against in tournaments and consider yourself a top recruit. Meanwhile, coaches scout not only those same athletes, but also thousands more throughout the country. That's why it's important to attend camps and showcases outside your region.

This reality check is not meant to destroy your dream, just alter it enough to make it more realistic and attainable. Remember that each school's needs can change from year to year. Priorities can change because of graduation, injuries, transfers, sub-par performances, or academic suspensions. There is a match for you somewhere in the country. Keep an open mind and do not neglect a school simply because of its name.

Hit the Web

Check out the web pages of your Target List schools and as many resources as possible. This will give you a feel for how important the athletic department is within the school's hierarchy and how important your sport is within the athletic department.

The school's web site will also tell you about the coaches, facilities, and the conference the school competes in. You should also check out the biographies of each athlete on the roster. It's a pretty good indicator of whether or not the coach recruits athletes like you.

Take your snapshot:

Ability
If you notice that most athletes on a team were All-State and you've only been awarded 2nd team All-League, that's a pretty good indicator that the talent level may be too high for you.

Physical Characteristics
How does your height and weight measure up to other athletes on the team?

Geography
Does the coach recruit nationally, regionally or is he satisfied with the in-state talent? Where are most of the athletes from?

Position
Is the team already stocked at your position? This may indicate that they have a great program for that position. However, it also may mean that they recruit the position heavily and thus it may take a couple of years before you are good enough to see in action.

Years of Eligibility
Do they expect everyone to graduate in four years? Does the conference allow graduate students to compete?

Junior College Transfers
Does the coach recruit "JUCO" transfers, who generally are more experienced and better athletes than high school graduates?

Over Stocking Athletes
Some coaches purposely over recruit athletes by position so they can "cherry-pick" from the surplus. A coach who does this may call the "extra" athletes into his office and "gently" urge them to consider enrolling at a JUCO until a spot opens up for them. This is a situation that is becoming more common.

"We look at the skill and talent level of all recruits to see how they would compete in our conference. We look for character as well as what our needs are, in terms of a specific position."
–Dermon Athlete, St. John's U., Assistant Basketball Coach, NCAA D-I

CASE STUDY:
How One Athlete Evaluated Schools for his Target List

Here is how one fictional athlete—Jason Kline—used the web to compare schools on his Target List. Using his physical attributes and high school statistics, he examined how he fit into two different collegiate baseball programs. Take a similar approach with your search, no matter what sport you aspire to play.

PERSONAL INFO

Name: Jason Kline
Height: 5-8
Weight: 150
Position: SS
B/T: R/R
Graduation: 2009
Hometown: Yorktown Heights, NY
School: Yorktown High School

2008 STATS

AVG	GP	AB	R	H	2B	3B	HR	RBI	BB	SO
.325	31	114	28	37	13	4	6	24	14	9

Bio

Jason is an outstanding shortstop entering his second full season on the varsity squad. Last year as a junior, Jason led the team in average and hits and was second in RBI. He also led the team in fielding percentage, committing just 1 error in 44 chances at short. Named team captain for his senior year, Jason will make a run at a second consecutive All-Section honor.

Goals

Upon graduation, Jason wants to play for a Division I program. He wants the opportunity to start at shortstop and have an immediate impact his freshman year. With this in mind, he's narrowed his Target List down to two schools.

Always enamored by Florida State, Jason grew up watching the Seminoles compete on television, he's aware of his father's success as the FSU third baseman ('71-'75). He would relish the opportunity to continue his father's legacy in an established collegiate baseball program.

He is also considering Quinnipiac U., a small Connecticut school. Quinnipiac is entering its tenth season as a Division I program and Jason sees this as a good place to bring his leadership qualities and grow with the program. Though completely different options, Jason sees advantages to both schools and is ready to "hit the web."

FLORIDA STATE UNIVERSITY'S BASEBALL ROSTER

Overall Record: 54-11-1 League Record: 19-5 National Ranking: #1
Head Coach: Mike Martin

No.	Name	Pos	B/T	HT	WT	YR.	Hometown
1	Tony McQuade	OF	S/R	6-2	205	SO	Gainesville, FL
2	Rocky Roquet	OF	R/R	6-2	195	FR	Anaheim, CA
4	Stephen Drew	SS	L/R	6-0	175	FR	Hahira, GA
5	Jerrod Brown	1B	L/R	5-10	200	JR	Auburndale, FL
7	Daniel Hodges	P	L/L	6-0	180	JR	Hilliard, FL
8	Michael Futrell	OF	R/R	6-0	180	SR	Tallahassee, FL
9	Kevin Richman	SS	S/R	6-0	160	FR	Clearwater, FL
10	Chris Hart	1B	S/R	6-1	190	JR	Clearwater, FL
13	Justin Miller	P	L/L	5-9	150	FR	Quincy, FL
14	Bryan Zech	2B	R/R	5-10	175	SO	Wellington, FL
15	Jeff Probst	2B/SS	R/R	5-10	175	SO	Clearwater, FL
16	Scott Toole	2B/3B	R/R	6-1	185	SR	Jacksonville, FL
17	Chris Whidden	P	R/R	6-0	175	JR	Tallahassee, FL
18	D. Davidson	P	L/L	6-4	215	JR	Panama City, FL
19	A. Cheesman	C	R/R	5-10	190	FR	Sarasota, FL
20	Robinson	OF	R/R	6-1	190	FR	D. Bar, CA
21	Blair Varnes	P	R/R	6-2	200	SR	Pascagoula, MS
22	Jason Newlin	P	R/R	6-0	185	JR	Tallahassee, FL
23	Tony Richie	C	R/R	6-1	210	SO	Jacksonville, FL
24	Eric Roman	P	R/R	6-2	195	JR	Orlando, FL
25	Nick Rogers	OF	R/R	6-1	195	SR	Vedra Beach, FL
26	Kevin Lynch	P/3B	L/R	6-2	185	FR	Ft. Pierce, FL
27	R. Barthelemy	3B/1B	L/R	6-3	230	SR	Miami, FL
29	Richie Smith	OF	L/R	5-11	200	SR	Bristol, FL
30	Robby Read	P	R/R	6-2	195	JR	Tallahassee, FL
31	M. LaMacchia	P	R/R	6-0	190	SO	Palm Harbor, FL
32	Blair McCaleb	C	R/R	6-0	205	SR	Marietta, GA
35	Brent Marsh	P	R/R	6-3	185	FR	Tallahassee, FL
43	Trent Peterson	P	R/L	6-1	180	SO	Tallahassee, FL
46	Matt Lynch	P	L/L	6-2	185	JR	Ft. Pierce, FL

Relevant Numbers

- 31 athletes on roster
- 8 freshmen
- 6 sophomores
- 10 juniors
- 7 seniors
- 6 of the freshmen are position athletes, 2 pitchers
- 25 are from Florida
- 3 SS on roster: (2 freshmen, 1 sophomore)

Here is Jason's evaluation of Florida State. Remember, this is based on his profile and goals. You may have a different outlook.

Things to consider...

- Nationally recognized as one of country's top programs.
- Incredible facilities, fields, road trips, etc.
- 3 SS on the roster—all are freshmen and sophomores so I'd probably need to change positions to have a chance at seeing time.
- Coach recruits primarily from Florida—very few out-of staters on roster.
- Will have to compete against some of country's top athletes for a roster spot.
- All athletes on roster have more accolades than I do.
- All athletes on roster are taller and heavier than I am.
- Will most likely have to make team as a walk-on.
- Too far for parents/friends to attend my games.
- Would be a dream to experience College World Series televised on ESPN.
- Many pro scouts follow the team.

QUINNIPIAC UNIVERSITY'S BASEBALL ROSTER

Overall Record: 17-24 League Record: 14-13 National Ranking: #278
Head Coach: Dan Gooley

No.	Name	Pos.	B/T	Ht.	Wt.	YR	Hometown
1	Avery, Keith	OF	R/R	5-10	170	JR	Trumbull, CT
2	D'Elia, Charles	SS	R/R	5-11	165	SR	Neponset, NY
3	Bennett, Dave	P	R/R	6-0	170	SO	Fairfield, CT
4	Puccio, Sal	1B/3B	R/R	6-1	205	SR	Brightwaters, NY
5	Jasilli, John	IF/P	R/R	5-11	155	SR	Brooklyn, NY
7	Marano, Albert	OF	R/R	5-10	170	SO	Lincoln, RI
8	Zides, Andy	IF	R/R	5-8	175	JR	Canton, MA
9	Silverstein, St.	C	R/R	5-8	160	SO	Merrick, NY
10	Bengel, Richard	P	L/L	5-11	175	SO	New Bern, NC
11	Abrahams, Dan	OF	R/R	5-7	140	SO	Great Neck, NY
13	Melillo, John	P	R/R	5-10	190	JR	Wethersfield, CT
14	Garrett, Robert	C/1B	R/R	6-2	200	JR	Brookfield, CT
19	Magee, Brian	OF	L/R	6-2	200	SR	Stamford, CT
20	Spahr, Mike	P	R/R	6-2	205	FR	Oceanport, NJ
21	LaPointe, T.	IF	R/R	6-0	190	JR	West Haven, CT
24	Rankowitz, K.	C	R/R	6-0	185	SO	Barrington, RI
25	Stonaha, Chris	3B	R/R	6-0	175	SO	Stratford, CT
30	Lavigne, Seth	OF	R/R	6-3	240	JR	Tolland, CT
31	Kafka, Ari	P	R/R	6-5	215	FR	Sharon, MA
32	Ellis, Jackson	P	R/R	6-1	190	JR	Ludlow, VT
33	Vartuli, Chris	C	R/R	6-0	190	SO	Norwalk, CT
36	Gresh, Chris	P	R/R	6-1	220	FR	Jewett City, CT

Relevant Numbers

- 22 athletes on roster
- 3 freshmen
- 8 sophomores
- 7 juniors
- 4 seniors
- All 3 freshmen are pitchers
- 15 are from NY/CT/NJ
- 1 SS on roster (a senior)

Here is Jason's evaluation of Quinnipiac.

Things to consider...

- ◆ Not known for their baseball program.
- ◆ Coach recruits from the northeast.
- ◆ Small school, less pressure.
- ◆ 1 SS on the roster and he's graduating.
- ◆ Good chance to play a lot of freshman year.
- ◆ Athletes on roster have accolades more in line with mine.
- ◆ Less competition for a starting position.
- ◆ Average athlete on roster is roughly my size.
- ◆ School is closer to home so family/friends can watch me play.
- ◆ No freshmen position athletes on roster—may have to wait until sophomore year to start.
- ◆ All 3 freshmen on the team are pitchers.
- ◆ Smaller roster means fewer spots available, fewer scouts, fewer road trips, etc.
- ◆ Cold weather climate—can't play outside year-round.

Final Analysis

You can learn a lot about how you fit in with a particular program just by evaluating their roster on-line. However, a roster from one particular year is not proof of a trend and some media guides inflate the accomplishments (and even height and weight) of their athletes to make their program appear more prestigious.

As always, the bottom line is that there is no substitute for going the extra step after your initial research is done. Reach out to coaches, athletes and recent graduates, and search the web for results of tournaments and conference championships. Be as knowledgeable as possible on each college you are considering.

Watch for Red Flags

A couple of red flags we need to make sure you are aware of when investigating athletic programs of schools on your Target List. If you notice a team you're interested in has only a few juniors and seniors on the roster (or vice versa), inquire about the following:

- ◆ How many athletes compete all four years?
- ◆ Do many quit after their first or second season?
- ◆ How many athletes receive diplomas?
- ◆ Do athletes suffer an unusually high number of injuries?

STEP 3 - Finalize Your List

You now should have two versions of your Target List, one with schools in order of academic preference and the other in order of athletic preference. See if you can combine the two lists without dramatically changing the order of either one. If one or more of the schools are in the top 10 of both lists, you've got yourself a great indicator of which schools you should focus your attention.

FINISH LINE: You now know how to do it, so it's time to build those lists. Using the information in this chapter, and the information from the previous chapters as well, begin to build your lists of schools based on academics and athletics. Then, compare the two lists, and you've begun to target schools that are a good all-around match for you.

Academic Schools   Athletic Schools

_____   _____

_____   _____

_____   _____

_____   _____

_____   _____

_____   _____

_____   _____

_____   _____

_____   _____

_____   _____

_____   _____

_____   _____

_____   _____

CHAPTER 5

ESSENTIAL ACTION STEPS TO TAKE

In This Chapter

- ◆ Different ways to promote yourself
- ◆ How and when to make campus visits
- ◆ Information on recruiting services
- ◆ When it's a good idea to try out as a walk-on

So far in this Guide, you've learned how college coaches look at the recruiting process, where you can get help, how to improve your profile to generate interest, and how to make a Target List of colleges you want to attend. Now, it's time to take action.

This chapter will cover a variety of steps you can take to make sure college coaches are aware of you, take an interest in you, and, as a result, help you get admitted to the school of your choice.

PROMOTING YOURSELF

Apply To Strong Academic Schools

As you might suspect, college coaches frequently ask admission officers to admit student-athletes who might otherwise not qualify academically or are "on the bubble." Of course, this does not mean a student whose academic profile is significantly below the school's minimums will be accepted simply at the coach's request.

However, if you are within a reasonable distance of a school's SAT/ACT and grade requirements, and are an athlete the coach wants on his squad, the coach probably has a good shot at getting you if he pushes hard enough.

A good rule of thumb to use is that your athletic ability should be able to get you into one school above where you would be accepted on academics alone.

At some schools, admission requirements may not be as stringent for recruits as they are for non-athletes. An Ivy League school may require students to possess at least a 3.6 GPA, yet a sought-after athletic recruit may only need to have a 3.4 GPA.

Remember, coaches at strong academic schools seek good athletes just like their counterparts at the top D-I programs. Their sports programs have every bit as much tradition and history, sometimes even more than the big D-I schools. And when you graduate, you have an excellent chance of obtaining a great job or being admitted to a graduate school of your choice.

Also, you have a much better chance of competing in college athletics by being a big fish in a small pond if you include some smaller or low profile schools on your list. For example, if your Target List features the U. of Florida (a national D-I powerhouse) where thousands of athletes may apply, and the college of William and Mary (a lesser-known school with an excellent athletic program and academics) where hundreds of athletes may apply, where is it easier to stand out? It's obvious—the statistics favor you at the smaller school.

The bottom line: use the athletic talents you have worked so hard to develop to give yourself a shot at getting accepted to one of the academic "reach" schools on your Target List. You owe it to yourself to pursue the best possible academic education available.

Don't focus on a school primarily for its athletic reputation. Years later this will just be another word on your diploma. Would you rather ride the bench at a well-known school or play for four years at a smaller school?

Coaching Communication

This is a vital part of getting into the school you want to attend. If you are academically on the border of being accepted to your top school, you'll want the head coach and his staff on your side. In many situations, they will have pull in the admissions office and willing to go out of their way to help out. You also want to begin learning about the coach's particular philosophy and overall strategy as early as possible. This information will help you decide where you want to continue you athletic and academic career.

Initiating Contact

Before your sophomore season, compile a broad list of schools you would most like to attend. Visit each of these schools' athletic websites to see if there is an online questionnaire that you can complete. Take your time to list all of your accomplishments. Be proud of your athletic career. There is no need to be modest, but never lie! Double check all the information you enter, especially your contact information. If you think your e-mail address may be inappropriate (partyanimal232@example.com, sexygirl37@example.com), create an acceptable one with a subtle indication of yourself (CHSlacrosse2@example.com or longjumper17@example.com). This can be done for free at hotmail.com, gmail.com, and yahoo.com.

Following Up
If you do not hear back from the coach right away, do not worry! He will likely enter you into a pool of potential recruits for the coming year. If you do not receive general information from the college via e-mail or snail mail within a month, you may want to write a brief, handwritten note to the coach politely asking if he received your questionnaire. This is also a good opportunity to inform him of any upcoming camps or showcases you will attend, and also include a copy of your team schedule.

Let Coaches Know You're Interested
During your junior year, send a letter of interest to each head coach on your Target List. The purpose of the letter of interest is to let the coach know that you would like to attend his school for academic reasons and to compete for his team.

It is extremely important to personalize your letter of interest. You will get even more mileage out of a handwritten letter. Make sure you spell the coach's name and address correctly, and include something specific about his team (i.e., team's record, top rivals, great facilities) so he knows your interest is based on knowing something about his program.

One cardinal rule: whether your letter is handwritten or printed from a computer, do not send a coach a photocopied letter. How would you feel receiving a letter that pretends to be written to just you, when it's obvious that same letter has also been sent to many others?

You feel like the sender has no idea who you are and doesn't really care, right? You want a coach to understand that you have genuine and specific interest in his school and that you have devoted a lot of time to researching his program. So make each letter of interest an original, from start to finish!

Begin the letter by explaining your interest in the school's academic program. Mention the major you will pursue or ones that interest you. Perhaps the school boasts some prominent professors whose classes you'd like to attend, or famous graduates who had similar interests to yours.

Discuss your educational and career goals, leadership ability, and your personal values. These characteristics demonstrate to the coach that you are well-rounded and that you plan on staying in school all four years. Avoid the temptation to discuss only athletics in your letter. Athletes who treat academics just as seriously as sports really impress coaches.

Don't forget to emphasize your athletic accomplishments and why you can contribute to the team.

- Let the coach know that you have a video available if he would like to see you in action.
- Do not send your video unless a coach specifically asks for it.
- Request literature about the college, a media guide, any camps they may offer and a schedule.
- Mention you'd like to attend a home game.

Along with your letter of interest, you should also provide your personal statistics, which is discussed below, and a copy of your high school schedule in case the coach decides to send a recruiter to one of your games. Limit your letter of interest to one page (not including the schedule or profile).

Sample Letter of Interest to a Coach

JAMIE TEGLAS
10324 Town Walk Dr.
Yorktown Heights, NY 10598
Phone: 914-555-1000 E-Mail: jumpshot7@aol.com

Jan 3, 2009

Mr. Keith Kessinger
Head Basketball Coach
Carson-Newman College
2130 Branner Avenue
Jefferson City, TN 37760

Dear Coach Kessinger:

After I graduate from Yorktown H.S. this June, I am interested in attending Carson-Newman College. My goal is to graduate with a Pre-Med degree from your prestigious McCarthur School. I am writing to express interest in attending your school and more specifically, playing basketball next year.

As a three-year captain of my high school basketball team, I have developed the skills and leadership ability to contribute to your nationally ranked squad. Last season I was nominated to the All-Section Team while leading my team in points per game (27) and assists (11).

My interest in Carson-Newman College has always been strong. I have had the opportunity to attend seven of your games. In fact, two alumni from my high school, Jim Nicholson and Spencer Davis, played for your team in the late '90s.

Attached is an Athlete Profile that details my academic and athletic accomplishments. You'll notice that I take my studies just as seriously as I do basketball, and I'm confident that I will represent your program with distinction.

Please add my name to your prospect list and send me information about Carson-Newman's basketball program. I would especially like to see a copy of your media guide.

Good luck this season. Go Eagles!

Sincerely yours,

Jamie

Jamie Teglas

Write Your Athlete Profile

In addition to your upcoming schedule, you should also include a Athlete Profile of yourself with each letter of interest you send. This one-page résumé should contain personal information, such as your interests, jobs you have held, volunteer or community work you have done, as well as highlights of your academic and athletic accomplishments.

Sample Letter of Interest

JAMIE TEGLAS FORWARD CLASS '07

Address:	10324 Town Walk Dr.
Phone:	914-555-1000
E-mail:	jumpshot7@aol.com
DOB:	June 24, 1991
Height:	6'4"
Weight:	165 lbs.
SS#	102-24-2422

ACADEMIC

High School:	Yorktown High School
	17 Green Road
	Yorktown Heights, NY 10598
	914-232-9444
Graduation:	Class of 2009
GPA:	3.8 GPA (on a 4.0 scale)
Class Rank:	Top 10%
SAT:	1900 Total (600 math, 640 verbal, 660 writing)
Honors:	National Merit Scholar
	2nd place County Science Fair Competition
	Student Volunteer of the Month, Mothers Against Drunk Driving
Counselor:	Jim Ryan (ext. 343)

HIGH SCHOOL BASKETBALL

Coach	Jim Dobbs (ext. 432)
Awards:	Basketball, All Section
	Team Captain, '06–'07, '08–'09
2005-06 Stats:	27 points/game
	11 assists/game
	7 rebounds/game

REFERENCES

Summer Coach	Jim Haas (718-232-9453)
Trainer	Lasse Viren (212-555-2234)
Teacher	Deborah Klein - (ext. 232) - English AP
Employer	Calvin Hobbs - McDonalds (718-343-3453)
Volunteer	Mgr. Stacey Jackson - Mothers Against Drunk Driving (718-343-9343)

Thank You Note after a Campus Visit

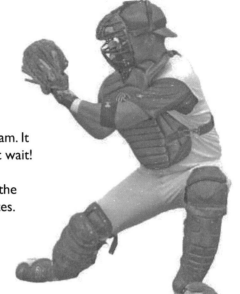

Dear Coach Kessinger:

Thank you for taking time to meet with me during my visit to Carson-
Newman College last Saturday. I really enjoyed touring the campus,
attending a science class, and speaking with you about your basketball team. It
gave me a great glimpse of what I can expect at college next fall. I cannot wait!

Watching the Eagles crush Wagner was awesome! I was impressed with the
talent of your squad, the team unity, and competitive spirit of your athletes.
I can definitely see myself wearing the Blue & Gold!

Thanks again for your hospitality and for your interest in recruiting
me.

Letter Providing New Information

Dear Coach Kessinger:

My high school basketball team is competing at the Nike High School Invitational in Tampa, Florida, December
7-10. If any of your assistant coaches are covering the event, I'd really appreciate it if they could watch me play.
Enclosed is the schedule, I'll be wearing #32.

By the way, I just found out that I made the Dean's List for the third semester in a row, and my research
project on solar energy won third prize in our county science fair. My hard work is paying off!

Thanks again for considering me for your 2009 recruiting class.

Telephone & E-Mail Contact

After you mail your letter of interest and Athlete Profile to coaches on your Target List, it is important for you
to maintain periodic telephone and/or e-mail contact with the school's coach. This will let him know that your
interest is strong and sincere. It will also give you an opportunity to evaluate where you stand on the recruiting
depth chart.

Make sure you have a purpose to each contact with a coach or school. For example, you can inform the
coach of an event you are attending, ask questions about the program, request information about the school
that cannot be found from published sources, or find out if the coach would like to see your highlight video.
Remember, it is illegal for NCAA coaches to call you or to return your phone calls until July 1 before your
senior year; however, they can e-mail you anytime.

You are permitted to phone and e-mail the coach as many times as you like. Just use common sense. The last
thing you want to do is annoy a coach by calling or e-mailing too often. One last bit of advice...you should place
the phone calls, not your parents. This will demonstrate that you are a mature and responsible young adult who
can speak on his own behalf.

Publish a Web Site

Once you are a high school junior, you should publish a personal web page at a free site like www.BeRecruited. com to give college coaches an easy and informative way to learn about you, follow your results, view bio info, references, grades, SAT scores, personal statistics, workouts or even your training log.

Go to the web page of each school on your Target List to find the e-mail addresses of the head coach and assistant coaches (some schools have as many as four different coaches and an administrative assistant who handles recruiting). Then e-mail each coach with a link to your web site and invite the coach to visit it periodically. Make sure to update your site frequently to encourage repeat traffic.

You can also find coach e-mail addresses using the free subscription you received with this guide at www. CollegeCoachesOnline.com.

If you decide to design your own website, here are some things to consider:

Ideas For Your Personal Web Page

- Keep the design and layout simple and easy-to-use. Don't make the coach work too hard to find information.
- Limit it to one page. Coaches are pressed for time, and too much navigating will discourage them from visiting.
- Include both academic and athletic information.
- Update the site regularly to keep it current—at least once a week during your season.
- Include multiple pictures of yourself in action.
- If you have the ability to include a short video clip, do it.
- Don't worry too much about fancy graphics. The coach is visiting for information, not entertainment.
- Make sure your results, personal statistics, height and weight, and any other information you provide is accurate.
- Avoid spelling or grammatical errors.
- Don't forget to email coaches to let them know the page is online.

Facebook, MySpace, and Other Social Web Networks

With the growing popularity use of social networking sites, be very careful what information and pictures you post for the general public. Make sure you always have an appropriate "default picture". This may be a coach's first impression of you after scouting you at a showcase, reading about you in the newspaper, or just hearing your name through the coaching grapevine. Make sure you use the privacy settings on your account to restrict sensitive information. If a coach requests access, carefully review all areas that may reflect you in a negative manner. Ask yourself, is this something my grandparents would find acceptable?

A good way to check-up on what is out there about you is to Google yourself, and be enter all of your name variations (Bill Smith, Billy Smith, Bill A. Smith, William Smith, William A. Smith). You may also want to expand this search to your email address.

By the same token, Google prospective coaches on your target list. You may learn some interesting stuff.

Press Clippings & Awards

Encourage your high school and summer league or club coaches to submit game results and photos to all media in your area. If they don't have the time to do this, ask if you could be in charge of publicity. When you

are mentioned online or in a newspaper, cut out the article and paste it on a sheet of paper.

Make enough photocopies for all the schools on your Target List and then go through each article with a yellow marker to highlight wherever your name appears. This will allow the coach to learn about your accomplishments quickly and easily.

Send the article to the coaches at each Target List school with a handwritten cover note like: "Dear Coach (insert name), I thought you might be interested in seeing this story. I look forward to speaking with you soon."

Questionnaires

Once a coach knows you're interested in his program, three important things will happen:

1. Your name will be entered in the team's recruiting database.
2. You will receive a questionnaire to complete.
3. You will receive the materials about the school.

The literature you receive will help you learn more about the school and its program and decide whether to keep the school on your Target List.

When your questionnaire arrives, complete it honestly. Avoid the temptation to exaggerate your academic or athletic accomplishments. If a coach discovers inconsistencies, he will remove you from his recruiting list. Also, let the coach know you are serious about his school by returning the questionnaire as soon as possible. Do not put it off!

Avoid the temptation to let your parents complete your questionnaires. If a coach notices an adult's handwriting or language on your form, he will assume you lack maturity and responsibility, and that your parents want the opportunity more than you do.

Avoid Rushing To Judgment

Do not reject a school too early in the process. Wait until you have thoroughly researched all of your options before telling a coach your interest level. It's difficult to predict how the recruiting process will evolve, and an offer you turned down in August may be your best or only option in April. If a coach makes the effort to contact you, respond promptly. Don't burn any bridges.

Emphasize Your Unique Selling Point

Although they hate to admit it, many selective colleges target certain groups of applicants for admission. They might want to increase the diversity of the student body, expand the physics department, or recruit a few potential future donors. To have the freshmen community they want, colleges need musicians and athletes, leaders in publications and student government, a certain percentage of alumni children, minorities, and international students.

Students in the targeted groups may have an easier time getting through the admissions process, and there is often special scholarship money available for people from certain backgrounds or who are interested in specific programs. So emphasize what is unique about you.

Prove How Badly You Want To Attend the School

Every time you visit a campus, meet an alumnus, or e-mail a professor, let the admissions office know. By rejecting students who have failed to show genuine interest, colleges can boost the percentage of accepted applicants who enroll. A high percentage of accepted applicants who enroll make schools appear more attractive, and it saves the cost of recruiting students and of "wooing" desirable students with generous merit aid.

A Strong Essay Can Make the Difference

Admissions deans often push hard for the writers of their favorite compositions. On the other hand, they also note the papers that are riddled with typos or grammatical errors. Generally speaking, typos reflect sloppiness. Even if you do have a tendency to be light on the spell check, there is no excuse for these kinds of errors. They can be eliminated entirely by careful and repetitive proofreading. Eliminate the mistakes and show you care about how you are perceived. Choose a topic you feel passionate about. Be creative!

On-Campus and Alumni Interviews Matter

Interviews are the only personal interaction in an otherwise paper-driven process. Admissions committees frequently consider whether or not you bothered to set this up, and what the interviewer thought of you. Aggressively seek out any official or unofficial representatives of your Target List schools. You never know which contact you make will be the one who will move your application from the "Rejected" to "Maybe" to "Accepted" category.

Take Advantage of Family Ties

If you have siblings, parents, uncles, aunts, or grandparents who attended a school on your Target List, give that school careful consideration because you have an edge there. Schools generally look favorably on relatives of students and/or alumni for obvious reasons—financial support, spirit, tradition, etc.—and this may give you a leg up over non-affiliated student-athletes who apply. Also, make sure to inform coaches if your father, mother or any of your siblings have competed at the college level.

Get Recommendations

Since most college coaches on your Target List are not going to see you compete in person, they will have to rely on recommendations from people they trust. It is extremely important to develop a network of credible and influential people who will provide recommendations. We suggest you ask the following people whom you know to write and/or call the college coaches on your Target List:

- High school coach
- Opposing high school coaches
- Any college coach or elite athlete in your sport
- Academy directors
- Influential alumni
- Camp directors/organizers
- Former teammates who competed in college

This is no time to be shy! Many adults are happy, if not flattered, to be asked to advocate for a young person who has taken the time to respectfully request their assistance. So ask. As we are sure you have heard many times before, the worst thing they can say is no.

When you ask people to write or call a college coach on your behalf, make sure they support you and feel you are college athletic material. Choose them carefully. Even one negative comment can be the "kiss of death."

GOING ON CAMPUS VISITS

Start Early

While campus visits are primarily junior and senior year events, there's no need to wait. Start visiting colleges as early as ninth grade. Take advantage of any chance to walk around a college campus. Check out schools near your hometown, stop by colleges during family trips, and visit older friends and siblings at school. The more visits you make, the better you will become at quickly sizing up a school, and recognizing what you want from a college.

"The campus visit is absolutely essential. You need to spend a night or two and talk to students and professors. You need to see how you would fit in and how comfortable you would be there."
—Joe Hannah, Swimming Coach, LeMoyne College, NCAA DII

Unofficial Visits

Starting in your freshmen year of high school, you should take unofficial visits to a variety of schools. Even though you are responsible for paying all of the travel expenses, it's a great way to get a good read on a school so you'll feel more confident when you develop your Target List a couple of years later. Make sure to let the coach know you are coming and that you want to stop by to introduce yourself. By making these visits regularly, you'll make a lasting and positive impression on the coaches whose help you may need come application time.

Pre-Plan Your Schedule

For unofficial visits, call the admissions office at least two weeks in advance to let them know you are coming to campus. An admissions counselor can tell you the dates and times for campus tours (they're usually held weekly), information sessions (a Q & A with an admissions office rep that takes place before the tour), and open houses (a day of events aimed at prospective students, scheduled once or twice a semester).

The counselor can also recommend classes to observe, help schedule individual meetings with faculty and coaches, provide out a campus map, a parking permit, and information on nearby lodging.

While it may not be the best resource for using in choosing your actual classes at college, www.ratemyprofessor.com will give you insight as to which professors are most liked by the student population. Use the school's website to see when they are teaching and try to sit in on both the best and worst liked professors.

Official Visits

Coaches extend official visit invitations to their top recruits so they can get to know the athletes better and promote their school's best features. Since official visits are an expense for the athletic program, only a limited number of athletes will receive these invitations.

If you're fortunate enough to receive one in your junior or senior year, it's an outstanding opportunity for you to evaluate everything about the college and determine if the school and team fit your needs. Most of the time, you will stay with other athletes on the team and eat meals with them. This gives you an excellent chance to ask lots of questions. Keep in mind:

- The NCAA allows you one expense-paid visit to five different schools. This restriction applies even if you are being recruited in two sports.

- Each visit may only last a maximum of 48 hours.
- You must provide college authorities with your official transcript and entrance exam scores.
- You may return to one of the schools you've already visited, but you must pay all expenses.
- You must be registered with the NCAA Clearinghouse for official visits to NCAA schools.

When to Go

The best time to visit is on a weekday not too close to the beginning of the semester and definitely not during finals week. That way, you'll see students and teachers going about their regular routines. This may go without saying, but pick a time when the weather is mild at the beginning of fall or end of spring so you can easily walk around and see how the students interact with each other outside of classes, the library and athletic department.

For some families, however, a weekend, summer, or winter break visit may be easier to schedule. While you obviously won't see an average day during those off times, you can still get a sense of the campus and the area. On a blitz tour of schools in a particular region, don't cram in more than two schools a day. It takes at least half a day to get an accurate feel for a campus.

Before Your Visit

Prior to your arrival, learn everything you can about the school. Read the school catalog and browse its web site. Think of questions to ask that are not answered in published materials. In other words, don't ask, "How many students go here?" Instead, ask questions like "What percentage of freshmen drop out?" and "Is there special academic tutoring for athletes?".

Decide beforehand what's important to you — anything from a strong political science department to single-sex dorms to a campus choir. Make a list of priorities and investigate them during your visit. Keep notes and ask the same questions at each school so you will have a means to compare them against each other.

What to Do On Campus

- Begin your visit with an information session and a campus tour.
- Sit in on a class.
- Check out the dorms.
- Eat in the cafeteria.
- Read the bulletin boards.
- Meet a faculty member and the coach.
- See the athletic facilities.
- Read the student newspaper.
- Try to find your favorite book on the library's computer system and then look for it in the stacks.

Remember to check out the area surrounding campus, too. What restaurants, stores, and recreation attractions are nearby? Police and fire stations, hospitals? How close is the bus or train station? Think about what you'd need to live around there: Bike? Car? Warmer clothes?

If you visit with your parents, roam the campus alone at some point for a taste of what it would be like in this new environment. If multiple tours are being help at the same time, which is often the case at open houses, then split up. Parents can use this time to meet with a financial aid officer.

Finally, check out the athletic facilities. Do they excite you? And by all means, watch the team practice or play a game. Can you visualize yourself as a member of this team?

Interviews

Some schools offer an interview with an admissions counselor as part of the campus visit. If you have an interview, don't be nervous. The interview is mostly just a chance for you to ask questions of a school official and show that you are interested.

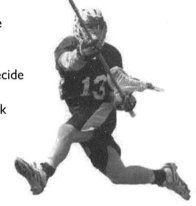

It's also an opportunity to make a positive impression on someone who may decide to go to bat for you in the applications process so make sure you're prepared, respectful, neat, and ask lots of questions. Dress nicely as this will make you look mature and respected. Also, research the school and have specific questions to ask. The counselor will take you seriously if you demonstrate you really want to be there. Some other tips: Arrive on time or a little early, make eye contact throughout the interview and be passionate when you speak.

Keep a Journal of College Visits

Keep a journal of your experiences. Take notes while you're on campus, jotting down the name of the dorm you walked through, the class you visited, and the names of professors and students you met (and their phone numbers and/or e-mail addresses, so you can contact them with follow-up questions). After each visit, write down your impressions — what you did and did not like about the school.

Take photos, to help you remember each campus when you're deciding where to apply. Make sure to write thank you notes to any school official who met with you individually.

Improper Recruiting Danger Signs

Most college coaches have your best interest at heart. However, you should be aware of improper recruiting tactics. Think twice if a coach:

- Tells you that your scholarship commitment is four years. Even though most coaches will renew your scholarship each year, they can only promise it one year at a time.
- Guarantees you an easy academic schedule and shows little interest in you as a student.
- Puts you in contact with a booster from the athletic department.
- Speaks negatively about other colleges you're considering.
- Offers you any monetary inducement, including college shirts or souvenirs.

Be sure to speak with your high school coach if you are concerned about any awkward situation. Do not jeopardize your eligibility by ignoring improper recruiting tactics.

Sample Questions to Ask Athletes on the Team

- How do you like the coaches?
- Is it difficult keeping up with your schoolwork?
- How much time do you devote to the team in the off-season?
- What don't you like about the program?
- How accessible are the academic tutors?

- How are the living arrangements?
- If you could do it all over again, would you still choose this school?
- Do all the athletes hang out together?
- How many hours per day do you study?
- What do you do socially?
- How do the professors and advisors treat athletes?
- How do the other students on campus feel about athletes?

Sample Questions to Ask the Coach

- Are you interested in recruiting me or will I have to walk-on? (Avoid the temptation to ask the coach if he is going to offer you a scholarship. If the coach is interested in you, he will bring it up. It's similar to going to a job interview. Would your first question be, "How much are you going to pay me?" Of course not!).
- What is the policy for walk-ons?
- What position do you see me playing?
- What is the off-season workout schedule?
- Will you red-shirt me?
- If I suffer an injury, become academically ineligible, or you decide I'm just not good enough for the team, what happens to my scholarship, if I have one?
- What are the graduation rates for athletes on the team?
- Am I eligible for any other sources of financial aid?
- Are there academic tutors available?
- How many athletes are on the roster? Are their backgrounds similar to mine?
- Does the team take any special trips?
- Am I expected to arrive earlier than the beginning of the school year?
- Which coach will be working with me the most?
- Are there any team rules or policies I need to be aware of?
- What equipment does the team provide for the athletes?
- Will I have required study hall hours?
- How often does the team lift weights and condition?
- Is this a full year commitment or can I play other sports?

Questions To Ask Yourself After the Visit

- Did the coach have bad things to say about the other schools that are recruiting me?
- Would I attend this school if I had no intention of competing there?
- Do the coaches and athletes get along and respect one another?
- Will I be successful academically at this school? Athletically? How do I measure up to everyone else?
- Were the coaches and athletes I met honest, friendly, and interested in me, or did they seem fake?
- Did the coaches stress academics? Did they ask me about my educational and career goals?
- Were they knowledgeable about my area of study? If not, did they introduce me to someone to answer my questions?
- Did I respect the coach and his philosophy?
- Will I fit in at this particular school?
- Do I have what it takes to commit to this coach and team for four years?
- Does the school satisfy all requirements that I identified earlier with my parents and counselor?

HIRING RECRUITING SERVICES

Why Recruiting Services May Not Be Effective

For a fee ranging from a couple hundred dollars to over $3,000, you can pay to have a recruiting service promote you to college coaches. They usually send a one-page profile and a highlight video to every school they feel is a good match. This could be several hundred schools or every school in the country.

The problem that coaches find with most recruiting services is that the person doing the evaluating is not credible, nor is it someone they personally know or respect. The evaluators tend to exaggerate your ability and project what level you can compete at by classifying you as a D-I, D-II, or D-III.

Categorizing athletes like this is flawed because the level of competition at each school varies so much within each division. In addition, the services bulk mail these profiles, so they are not personalized. This can be annoying for coaches.

Coaches feel some of these services can be a waste of money and that they take advantage of athletes. It's your job to do comprehensive research. Understand that receiving questionnaires or camp invitations from coaches after using a recruiting service does not necessarily mean you are being recruited. Ask questions like the ones below before you commit financially.

Questions to Ask The Recruiting Service Before You Register

- Who evaluates me and does he have a financial interest in how he rates my skills? In other words, is he a salesman or a scout? (An unbiased evaluation has the most credibility with coaches.)
- Can you guarantee me a scholarship? (This is impossible to do.)
- What kind of expertise do you have in my sport?
- Did you personally go through the college recruiting process?
- Can anyone use this service or do you have to possess the ability to compete in collegiate athletics? (The best services only accept athletes with college potential.)
- Can you provide the names and phone numbers of three athletes from my area who have used your service?
- What percentage of the athletes who use your service receive interest from college coaches?
- Have any coaches offered scholarships to athletes as a result of your service?
- Will you send my profile and video in its own envelope? (If it's sent with hundreds of others, it will not get the attention it deserves.)
- How many athletes receive no response even after all your promotion? (An honest service will tell you that most athletes do not receive interest from college coaches.)
- Do you offer a money-back guarantee?
- Which college coaches endorse your service?

What To Look For When Selecting A Recruiting Service

Choosing the right recruiting service to represent you to college coaches could mean the difference between continuing your athletic career or hanging up your uniform for good. Here are five criteria you should consider when choosing a company:

1. **Evaluators**
   Who is grading your skills? It is extremely important that a knowledgeable and respected coach writes your evaluation.

2. **Business History**
   How long has the company been in business? Are they an unproven start-up or have they been around for a while?

3. **Enrollment Procedure**
   Does the company represent any athlete who will pay its fee, regardless of ability? Make sure the service you choose limits enrollment to only athletes with college potential.

4. **References**
   Are they willing to provide names of athletes' parents you can call who have used their service in the past? If not, look elsewhere.

5. **Track Record**
   How many of their past customers competed in college? Did any receive scholarships? Also, don't be impressed by their All-American alumnus who signs with a top college. Blue chippers are going to receive attention regardless of the recruiting service.

TRYING TO MAKE THE TEAM AS A WALK ON

What Is A Walk-On?

A walk-on is a term used for an athlete who is not recruited but impresses the coaching staff during tryouts and is invited to join the team. Some teams are full of athletes who are not recruited. In fact many programs rely on walk-ons to keep their team competitive.

4 Different Types of Athletes Who Make Up a College Roster:

1. **Scholarship Athletes**
    These athletes are the blue chippers who are heavily recruited by many colleges and are expected to be major contributors immediately.

2. **Athletes Who Are Recruited But Are Not Given Athletic Scholarship Money**
    These athletes may also be heavily recruited but may not have the type of personal records to warrant athletic scholarship money. They usually receive many of the same benefits as the scholarship athletes like access to athletic housing, pre-registration for classes and in some cases, guaranteed admittance to the school.

    Some of theses athletes may have even received scholarship offers at other schools but turned them down to attend more competitive academic institutions. They are also expected to contributors but not as quickly as a scholarship athletes.

3. **Non-Recruited Athletes That Inform The Coach They Would Like To Walk-On**

    Many athletes are not recruited for various reasons. They may have been injured their senior year, they may be late bloomers or their statistics are just not good enough for the coaches to think they could contribute to the team. Fortunately, the recruiting process is not an exact science.

    There are many All-American certificates given to athletes who coaches didn't think were good enough to be recruited. Many walk-ons continue to develop through their college years and become stars while many recruited athletes never improve on their high school performances.

    If you intend to walk-on to a team, your best chance for success is to let the coach know of your intentions as soon as you gain admittance to the school. By doing this, the coach is able to follow your progress through your senior year.

    The coach may even recommend workouts that you can do over the summer to prepare yourself for the fall training schedule. In some cases, athletic housing spots may open up so you can room with another athlete. By notifying the coach of your intentions before school begins, you are showing a desire to compete, which any coach should respect. Even if a coach discourages you from walking-on, be persistent and show your commitment.

4. **Athletes Who Show Up On The First Day Practice And Ask To Walk-On**
    These athletes rarely make the team. By failing to notify the coach ahead of time, they do not show signs of being committed to the sport. In many cases, practice may have already been going for a week and at certain schools some teams have attended a pre-season camp.

ATTENDING SCHOWCASES

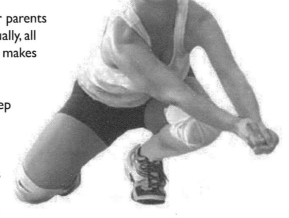

Showcases are usually one or two-day events that attract about 100 or more athletes who all desire to play college sports. Coaches and pro scouts from the region are invited to attend the workouts and evaluate each athlete's skills.

Most coaches are not allowed to communicate with athletes or parents at the event and they usually stand off to the side to watch. Usually, all of the coaches watch one athlete perform a task at a time. This makes showcases outstanding opportunities for exposure.

While every athlete's ultimate goal is an athletic scholarship, keep in mind that a showcase is only one step in a long recruiting process. Very rarely will a coach make a scholarship offer after one event. The best time to start attending showcases is during your sophomore or junior year of high school. This gives coaches a chance to follow your progress through high school if you impressed them, and it gives you valuable experience in a tryout environment.

"I get about 150 letters each year and I can't go through them all. I like to see each athlete compete myself. In that respect, the showcases are great because it helps to cut through a lot of the fat. Occasionally, we do miss top athletes. However, in this day and age, with all those showcases, you would have to live at the North Pole for us not to find you."
- Jeff Albies, Head Baseball Coach, William Patterson U., NCAA D-III

College Coaches Like To Recruit At Showcases Because They Can...

♦ Evaluate many athletes in a short amount of time, especially those that have shown a genuine interest in attending their school.
♦ Save money — showcases are cost-effective and allow coaches to consolidate their recruiting trips.

You Should Attend Showcases Because You Can

♦ Be seen in action by many coaches at one time.
♦ Evaluate how your ability compares to others from your region.
♦ Get an unbiased and professional opinion of your ability. After the showcase, make sure to ask the director for your scores.
♦ Determine your "recruitability." You will know you made an impression if you receive letters or phone calls from coaches who attended the showcase a few weeks later.
♦ Receive experience competing in a pressure-filled environment. The more showcases you attend, the calmer and more relaxed you will be when they really count (during the summer and fall of your senior year).

Questions To Ask the Showcase Director Before Registering

♦ Which coaches have committed to attend? (The biggest problem with showcases is that it's hard to predict exactly which coaches will show up since they are not paid to attend.)

- Which coaches have attended the event during the last two years?
- How many athletes will attend the showcase?
- What is the format?
- How many athletes in the past have received interest or scholarships from coaches as a result of attending the showcase?
- Are there games? If yes, how much playing time can I expect?
- Do you provide references? (If so, make sure to call them!)
- Is there a refund in case of bad weather?
- Will I receive college or pro instruction at the event?

Follow-Up With Coaches

E-mail the coaches who attended the showcase and ask for their advice regarding what areas of your game need improvement and what kind of schools might need an athlete of your ability. Most coaches, regardless of their recruiting interest in you, will have notes from the showcase rating your ability. You never know who can help you. The more people you ask, the more opportunities you will have. Be aggressive!

What Not To Expect

College coaches will probably not do any of the following things at a showcase:

- Announce themselves. Most coaches like to remain anonymous to prevent awkward conversations with athletes and parents.
- Offer you a scholarship at the event. The showcase is only one step in a long evaluation process.
- Expect you to perform perfectly. In fact, they want to see how you react after you make a mistake. Coaches are there to evaluate your skills and project what level they feel you could compete at in two or three years.
- Treat you any differently because of your past accomplishments. Everyone gets the same opportunity to shine.
- Talk to you or your parents. If coaches are interested in you, they will follow up with a phone call or letter.

Tips for Making the Most of Your Showcase Experience

Inform Coaches That You Are Attending the Showcase

Write or e-mail coaches on your Target List, as well as coaches expected to attend and tell them you will be participating in the showcase. Even if some of the schools on your list are located far away, the coaches may want to inform their local scouts to stop by and check you out. It's easy to e-mail. But remember, a hand written note goes a lot farther with a coach at a school you are truly interested in.

Dress In a Full Uniform

It is important that you look like an athlete. If possible, wear a jersey with your name on the back so it is easy for a coach to identify you from the 100 or so other athletes attending. First impressions are crucial so wear a clean uniform, tuck your jersey in, and leave the jewelry at home.

Hustle

Hustle at all times, even if others don't. You never know who is watching. More important than ever before, give 100%.

Get Evaluated At Multiple Positions

Ask to be evaluated at every position that you play well. This will give coaches a chance to see more of you during the day. Also, you may be set on one primary position, but a coach may see more potential for you somewhere else. You are a more attractive recruit if you are versatile.

Spend Every Minute of Downtime Wisely

Since only one person is usually evaluated at a time, you will spend a lot of time on the sidelines waiting for your turn. If coaches are interested in you, they may want to keep an eye on you during these times. Don't fool around on the sidelines with your friends.

Instead, if it is allowed, use the downtime to practice. You will give interested coaches another opportunity to scout you. When you're on the field or court, never sit.

Act like an athlete from the minute you arrive. There are coaches, recruiters and scouts who will want to watch you at all times. They will make negative notes if you have your parents run errands or you act disrespectful. Carry your own equipment and don't have your parents do it.

Cheerlead

If others make great plays or need some encouragement, cheer them on. Coaches will be impressed by your team spirit and leadership ability. A great way to be seen as a leader is to encourage teammates when they make a mistake, instead of berating them or criticizing them. Coaches are favorable to these kinds of athletes.

Attitude

Attitude is extremely important! It's not so much how an athlete handles himself during success, but how he react to failure. If you make a mistake or error, don't slam your equipment or exhibit negative body language.

Instead, move on in a composed manner. Use this opportunity to show your mental strength when faced with adversity. The coach knows you made a mistake and wants to see how you handle it emotionally and mentally.

Also, your actual results during a showcase or tryout aren't as important as you might think. Most recruiters are observing your skills and not so much what you do. They're trying to project where you might be athletically in a couple of years. If you show the right mechanics and have quick times in drills, that's more important than if you scored a goal, hit a home run or scored twenty points.

They want to compare your skills to athletes you'll compete against in college, not so much what you did that day. A 6'5" athlete at a basketball showcase, might score at ease, but the coach will evaluate his footwork, for instance, and estimate how he will perform against other college athletes his height.

Get Dirty

Coaches love to recruit athletes who are not afraid to be extra aggressive. Just be sure that your hustle isn't "fake hustle." A shortstop who dives for a grounder fifteen feet away and clearly out of his reach is showing the wrong kind of hustle and a coach will spot that easily.

If No One Shows Interest In You

Do not assume that just because none of the attending coaches expressed interest in you after the showcase that you cannot compete on the college level. Keep this in mind:

- Most coaches attend showcases with specific recruiting needs in mind. The coaches in attendance might not have a need for an athlete at your position.
- Coaches could be extremely impressed with your ability, but notice your GPA and test scores are too low. In this case, they cross you off their list, no matter how skilled you are.
- The coaches who attended the showcase are only a very small sample of college teams. Remember, there are thousands of teams you can choose from.
- There are lots of other showcases to attend. The more coaches that see you play, the better chance you will have of generating interest.

When you attend a showcase, your every move is being evaluated. Here are some things that you should avoid:
- Arriving late.
- Acting like you're a star or big man on campus.
- Wearing a baseball cap backwards.
- Asking your parent to carry your bags or get you water.
- Wearing earrings, bracelets, a watch, or a pony-tail.
- Getting upset if you don't perform well.
- Asking the showcase evaluators your scores before the event is over.
- Not listening
- Complaining or speaking negatively within earshot of anyone you don't know.

The Showcase Showdown
Joshua Lyons, Ft. Lauderdale, FL

It's not necessarily who you know, but rather, who knows you that's important. This is the mentality I took when deciding to showcase my talent for college coaches. My .417 BA and 14 HR during my junior year of high school spoke for itself, but I needed to do more. I knew what my potential was, and now it was time for college coaches to find out for themselves. Attending a few showcases was the answer. I suited up for two showcases here in Florida, and made the trip to North Carolina for another.

I was pretty nervous for the two local showcases, but I calmed down and played really well up north. However, in Florida, I got the chance to see how I compared to other kids from my area. Plus, with many top coaches and scouts in attendance, I got great exposure.

When I got back from North Carolina, I got letters and phone calls from coaches who saw me play. It was nice to have coaches show interest in me rather than the other way around.

Eventually, I accepted an offer from a coach who saw me play here in Florida. He knew I was going to North Carolina and had another coach follow me there. He was impressed with my effort when he first saw me and wanted another opinion. I didn't even know he was sending someone to scout me. I guess you never know who is watching.

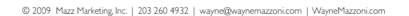

PRODUCING A HIGHLIGHT VIDEO

A highlight video allows coaches who do not get an opportunity to see you compete in person evaluate your skills accurately. By watching your video, coaches can assess your abilities personally and decide if you're a prospective recruit. They don't have to rely on someone else's evaluation who may be biased.

At a recent U. of Tennessee baseball camp, a parent asked Head Coach Rod Delmonico what kind of importance he places on highlight videos. He explained how helpful they are when judging the athlete's on-field ability but warned against producing amateur-looking footage.

While it isn't always necessary to hire a professional production company, the tape should have a "professional feel" to it. Parents should not be overheard cheering in the background, and the camera should remain steady and in focus. Little distractions like these could strip the video, and the athlete, of all credibility.

Coaches are not critiquing your video editing skills; so don't worry about making yours look like a segment on ESPN Sports Center. If you are concerned about producing your own video, you can hire professionals, who will do everything for you. If you choose to save the money (some companies will charge you $500 or more!) and do it yourself, follow these steps:

1. Use a combination of practice and game footage.
2. Wear a full uniform so you look like an athlete.
3. Get right to the action! Edit out all dead time periods.
4. Limit the length of the tape to four minutes. Coaches will not watch long videos. Less is better.
5. Use a tripod at all times so the camera doesn't shake.
6. Tell the cameraman or anyone within earshot to avoid "cheerleading." The only sound should come from competition.
7. Make sure to shoot from angles that coaches want to see.
8. If you have access to video-editing software, you can shoot all the footage and edit it at home on your computer. If you don't, you will need to record over clips you do not want to include. The video should only feature your best performances.
9. Convert the video to DVD format and make as many copies as you need (check with the coach to see which he prefers, you may even be able to just e-mail the file or upload it to an online source). Use a sticker to label the video with your name, graduation year, position, address, and phone number. Make sure to write the title.—i.e. "Jeff Wilson's 4-minute highlight tape ('09 Grad)"

Introduction

Place the camera on a tripod a few feet away and introduce yourself. Speak clearly and confidently. Practice so it sounds conversational and not like you're reading a script. Include:

- Full name and graduation year
- High school's name and your coach's name
- City and state where you live
- Height and weight and Position(s)
- SAT/ACT scores and GPA
- Rank in class
- What you want to study in college (if you're undecided, it's okay to say you're undecided, but just mention some of your interests at this point like liberal arts or business)

Make sure you put all of your contact information—your full name, position, address, phone number—on a sticker on the outside of your video.

It's very possible that this video might get separated from the rest of your materials in a college coach's office, and you don't want the coach to get you mixed up with another recruit. Remember, the easier you make it for the coaches, the more open they will be to you.

TRAVEL, ALL-STAR & SELECT TEAMS

Research needs to be done to determine which travel, all-star, or select teams to try out for to gain the maximum quality of experience and exposure, and which college camps are best for you.

Many of these teams don't attract coaches to their games. The same holds true for showcase camps. Some of these camps may be expensive, but don't really provide an effective showcase for the athlete. It's imperative to do your research before you invest your time and money.

All teams are not created equal. In recent years, the number of athletes wanting to participate have grown enormously, diluting the talent base. Just about anyone can create such a team. With the growing number of athletes, there is a growing demand for these teams. This allows just about anyone to say "Hey, let's start a travel team" and many people do.

Determine if a particular team is truly made up of above-average athletes and if it competes against the kind of competition that a college coach views as superior. If you have begun communication with coaches, ask them to recommend any teams to you. Also, when looking at team rosters of your Target Schools, keep an eye out for former teams the athletes have been on.

One test to determine if the team you're considering is a true select team is to gauge the competition. If it's mostly local and their schedule is fairly indiscriminate, chances are it's not a bona fide select team. Some parents may pick teams that are "select" in their eyes only.

Also, just because a team "travels" does not mean that it is an elite one, composed of superior athletes. A true select team is composed of the caliber of athletes and plays the level of competition that regularly attracts college and pro scouts.

It is good to get out and have fresh competition, but do the research so you don't waste time or money playing against athletes who are underdeveloped. If college coaches don't attend at least a few games to scout athletes, it may not be the best team to get noticed.

What Is Their Focus?
Is it primarily to prepare athletes (the younger aged teams) for high school ball? If so, that might not give you the exposure you're looking for. A true select team very likely takes the assumption, based on the quality of athletes selected, that your high school tryout will most likely be the easiest tryout you'll have.

How Many Games Do They Play?
If they play relatively few games, especially in a cold climate, then they probably aren't a bona fide select team. If you're a baseball athlete in Indiana, for instance, and the team you're considering only plays 20 games in a season, that's not nearly enough to gain the experience an athlete from Florida or Texas will have, who will play at least twice as many games.

Who Do They Play?
Is their competition high-level competition or are you aware of other teams that play much tougher opponents.

Who Coaches The Team?

Is it the father of one of the athletes? Many of the best select teams don't allow parents to coach their own offspring (for obvious reasons). Also, is the coach paid or does he work on a volunteer basis? Also, what are the coach's qualifications? Did he play or coach college or professionally?

What's The Team Practice-To-Games Ratio?

If it's all games and only a few or no practices, it may still be a good quality team, but teams that don't practice much, don't really teach much, either. At younger levels, the practice-to-games ratio is more important.

How Many Athletes Make The Team?

If the number is so large that it's obvious several athletes aren't going to get much playing time, then that team might not be a good fit. A baseball or softball team carrying 16 athletes means that at a lot of those athletes probably will log a lot of pine time.

It's more important to play a lot for a lesser team than sit on the bench for a more prestigious team.

What If I Can't Make A Select Team or Can't Afford One?

Don't worry. Sometimes it's just not practical or possible to be on such a team. If, for any reason, you can't get on a select team, then make up for it in other ways—more practice on your own or private coaching. Nothing can replace dedication and hard work.

FINISH LINE: This was a long and information-packed chapter, and one that you'll no doubt want to refer back to on many occasions.

Now that you have all this information about how to take an active role in your recruitment, it's time to get started. Here's a quick checklist of things you can begin doing:

- ◆ Prepare your written profile.
- ◆ Send out Letters of Interest to the schools on your Target List.
- ◆ Publish a web page for yourself.
- ◆ Plan and take campus visits.

CHAPTER 6

DRIVE DOWN THE COST OF COLLEGE

In This Chapter

* NCAA scholarships by sport for D1 & D2 programs
* Where to find scholarship money outside of athletics
* How to determine how much money you need and your "family contribution"
* Various types of financial aid and when forms should be submitted
* Tips for receiving a good aid package and where to find loans

This chapter may have you scratching your head. After all, if a goal of this Guide is to help you get an athletic scholarship, why do you need to worry about paying for college?

Well, as we've said before, athletic scholarships are difficult to obtain and most don't cover all of your costs.

Even if you're the next superstar, the chances are good you're going to have to pay for at least some of your college expenses and possibly locate other sources of money to assist you and your parents with the upcoming costs.

NCAA SCHOLARSHIPS BY SPORT

The following table lists the allowable number of scholarships for NCAA divisions I and II. This does not suggest that each college program offers the full amount of possible scholarships for each sport. That decision is governed by each school's sports budget and other factors.

NCAA DIVISION I

Sport	Men's	Women's
Baseball/Softball	11.7	12
Basketball	13	15
Track & Field	12.6	18
Football	85	0
Golf	4.5	6
Gymnastics	6.3	12
Field Hockey	0	12
Ice Hockey	18	18
Lacrosse	12.6	12
Swimming/Diving	9.9	8.1
Tennis	4.5	12
Volleyball	4.5	12
Water Polo	4.5	8
Wrestling	9.9	0

NCAA DIVISION II

Sport	Men's	Women's
Baseball/Softball	9	7.2
Badminton	0	10
Basketball	10	10
Bowling	0	5
Track & Field	12.69	12.69
Fencing	4.5	4.5
Football	36	0
Golf	3.6	5.4
Gymnastics	5.4	6
Handball	0	12
Field Hockey	0	6.3
Ice Hockey	13.5	18
Lacrosse	10.8	9.9
Rifle	3.6	7.2
Rowing	0	20
Skiing	6.3	6.3
Squash	9	7.2
Swimming/Diving	0	9
Sync. Swimming	0	5
Tennis	4.5	6
Volleyball	4.5	8
Water Polo	4.5	8
Wrestling	9	0

FACTS ABOUT FINANCIAL AID

Athletic Scholarships

Once again, we remind you that being realistic about the financial aspect of college is just as important as setting your admissions and athletic expectations. Next to purchasing a home, paying for college is the biggest investment you or your parents will likely face. Everyone in the family needs to be on the same page when anticipating expenses and how to reduce them.

Compare the costs of your Target Schools with our worksheet, "College Cost Comparisons," in Chapter 8.

Financial Aid Helps Roughly 75% of All Students Afford College

Simply put, as much as athletic and academic concerns should dictate your Target List schools, the price of college may ultimately have even more to do with where you end up. The cost of college is high and rising — tuition for four years averages $99,784 at a private college or $45,352 at a public university — so you should definitely consider applying for financial aid to help pay expenses.

Overall college costs can, and should be, an important consideration in your final selection process. With a little research and dedication, however, you can avoid having the expense of college dictate which schools you apply to. There are many ways to alleviate the financial burden, and you must employ a creative plan and investigate all areas of help.

Become familiar with all the sources of aid that are available to you, and constantly stay abreast of this ever-changing landscape. We urge you to speak with your guidance counselor and research on web sites like www.collegeanswer.com, www.collegeboard.com, www.scholarships.com, and www.fastweb.com.

Over 600,000 Scholarship Opportunities Available!

Fastweb.com, an internet scholarship search site, features information on over 600,000 different scholarships and aid programs. Even though it takes a lot of time and paperwork to win this "free" money, it could save your family a lot of money. That makes it well worth the effort. We've already explained how tough it is to get an athletic scholarship, and when you consider that NCAA D-I Ivy and Patriot League schools, all NCAA D-III schools, and all NJCAA D-III schools do not even offer athletic scholarships, you'll understand how important it can be to locate other aid.

Determine How Much Money You Need

Get out the calculator. Below is a list of general expense categories which are part of any college student's budget. To give you and your parents a general idea of how much money it will take to get you through college, estimate each of these categories. Add it all up, and you've got yourself a budget, which needs to be funded from one or more of the following: your parents, your savings and any scholarships or aid programs available to you.

Budget Categories for Your College Education:

- ◆ Tuition & Fees
- ◆ Room & Board
- ◆ Books & Classroom Supplies
- ◆ Personal Expenses
- ◆ Transportation

Many websites have a variety of guides and calculators, which let you plug in schools and numbers to come up with anticipated costs. Be sure to include a "safety" account in case of any emergencies that may arise while at school.

Family Contribution

Most colleges will expect you to contribute to your college expenses based upon your parents' annual income and their assets. When referring to the Family Contribution Schedule (see Chapter 8), you will need to know your parents' net assets and annual income before taxes.

Take the net assets and read down according to your family size until you get to your parent's annual income, and this will determine your family contribution. Subtract your family contribution from the college cost and the result will indicate the amount of aid that can be available.

Example: If your parents' net assets are $40,000 and their annual income is $44,000 for a family of three, then your family contribution will be $6,869. If the college cost is $15,000, then your aid eligibility would be $8,131.

Loans, Grants, Merit Scholarships, and Work-Study

So, where does the money come from to send you to school? It can come in the form of loans, grants, scholarships, and federal work-study grants. Need-based loans are granted through Perkins or Stafford loan programs. The federal government may also distribute loans to families who have trouble meeting their family contribution. Congress has two programs to assist families in this situation: the Parent Loans for Undergraduate Students (PLUS) and the Supplemental Loans for Students (SLS). More than 60% of all financial aid comes in the form of student loans.

You should be careful that your on-campus job is not so time-consuming that it detracts from your studies. Pick a job that allows you to sit at a desk. This will allow you to read, and possibly get work done while earning money. Just make sure you don't let this get in the way of fulfilling your job responsibilities. Also, be aware that, your athletic obligation will occupy a considerable amount of your free time.

Many need-based financial aid packages may include grants or scholarships. In addition, the college you attend may reward you with a special grant or scholarship for distinguished achievements within a particular area, such as academics or athletics.

The federal work-study program is designed to provide students with on-campus jobs. The jobs range from giving campus tours to filing books in the library. The money you earn in work-study is paid directly to you on a weekly or monthly basis depending upon the school. It can be used to help pay tuition, room and board, books, or any personal expenses.

Financial Aid Forms

To apply for financial aid, you will have to complete the Free Application for Federal Student Aid (FAFSA). The form can be downloaded from www.fafsa.ed.gov or you can get it from you local high school guidance counselor. It compiles all your family's finances and rates the information to determine your eligibility for aid. Other forms may include the FAF (Financial Aid Form), the SAAC (Student Aid Application for California), and the FFS (Family Financial Statement).

College Scholarship Service/Financial Aid Profile

Some colleges that offer institutional financial aid ask applicants to complete a "profile" in addition to the FAFSA. The profile requests much more comprehensive and detailed financial information. If asked to submit this form, you should do it, because it could lead to additional money for you. Call 800-778-6888 to register and an application packet will be mailed to you.

Timeline

Financial aid forms should be completed and submitted no later than February of your senior year so that you are eligible for assistance. By mid-April, you will receive an award letter from each school where you have been accepted. The packages will vary at each school and may include federal and state grants, school scholarships, student loans, and on-campus jobs. This will allow you to determine which school is offering you the best package.

The Relationship Between The Financial Aid and Admission Offices

Most schools claim that their admissions office and financial aid office are independent and do not influence each other's decisions. Usually, the best overall students are admitted regardless of their financial need, and the average students are evaluated based on how much money they will cost the school.

WHAT YOU NEED TO KNOW ABOUT LOANS

Student loans can be instrumental in making college education affordable, but remember all loans must be paid back. Usually you do not have to start paying your loans until you either graduate or leave college for an extended period of time. Before taking out a loan, make sure that you and your family understands the exact conditions.

Subsidized Loans

The federal government pays or "subsidizes" the interest on your loans while in college. This reduces the amount of money you have to pay back over the life of your loan. A subsidized loan is awarded on the basis of financial need.

Grace Period

All student loans have a six to nine month grace period between the time you leave college and the time you start paying back your loans. Even if you do not graduate from college, you will still be expected to repay your loans. The repayment period for parent loans begins shortly after the loan is disbursed.

Loan Deferment

If you have an emergency that prevents you from repaying your loan, you can request a temporary loan deferment so that you do not have to pay your loans during this time. You must apply and be approved before you can qualify for a loan deferment.

Promissory Note

When applying for a student loan you must sign a legal document where you "promise" to repay the loan plus the accrued interest.

Default

If you do not repay the loan according to the terms of the promissory note, you are in default, and your credit rating and eligibility for future financial aid will be jeopardized.

For more information on loans check out these websites:

Chela Financial	www.loans4students.org
Nel Net	www.nelnet.net
FinAid	www.finaid.org
Students.gov	www.students.gov

TERMS

FAFSA: Free Application for Federal Student Aid) Form you must complete in order to determine your eligibility to receive financial aid from any college in the U.S.

EFC: (Estimated Family Contribution) Based on the information on your FAFSA, this is the government's calculation of the amount your family can afford to contribute towards college expenses. Indicates financial need.

SAR: (Student Aid Report) includes your EFC and is sent to the colleges you listed on your FAFSA.

TAP: (Tuition Assistance Program) Provides New York State students who demonstrate financial need with grants that range from $100 to $5,000. Only New York State students who plan to attend college in New York are eligible.

HEOP/EOP: (Higher/Education Opportunity Program) Available at some public and private colleges in New York State. Provides financial and academic support for students who are educationally and economically disadvantaged.

FSEOG: (Federal Supplemental Educational Opportunity Grant) Awarded to students who demonstrate exceptional need. Limited and only distributed by some colleges. Grants range from $100 to $4,000 per year.

Pell Grants: Federal grants that range from $400 to $4,000 per academic year and are awarded to students who demonstrate financial need.

FWS: (Federal Work Study) Awards college jobs to students to earn money to pay various school-related expenses.

CSS Profile: (College Scholarship Search Profile) Financial aid form required by many private colleges. There are registration and other fees associated with this form.

APTS: (Aid for Part-Time Study) Awarded to part-time students who live and attend colleges in new York State. APTS provides grants of up to $200 per academic year.

TIPS FOR RECEIVING THE BEST PACKAGE

Apply to Expensive Schools, Even If You Need a Lot of Aid

If an expensive college sees you as a desirable candidate, you should definitely apply, regardless of your financial situation. As long as you have a financial need, the school will provide the money you need. Believe it or not, you could actually pay less to attend a high-tuition private school than a lower cost state school. Knowing that your family contribution can be roughly the same at schools with varying costs will enable you to concentrate on non-financial considerations in selecting schools to apply to.

If your parents' income is too high and you do not qualify for need-based aid, you may find that merit aid puts a high-sticker school within reach. Colleges are awarding more merit aid packages in order to attract higher-caliber students. Most colleges are able to meet the financial needs of all of their students, but keep in mind that a lot of packages feature mostly federal loans and work-study and fewer grants. And that means you will be paying off these loans for years to come.

Request a Better Deal At Your First-Choice School By Playing Colleges Against Each Other

Most aid administrators agree that if you don't get the aid you think you need, you should appeal your case. Your circumstances may warrant a second look, or a mistake on your applications could come to light. Frequent mistakes include claiming college expenses for a sibling who has dropped out and stating your adjusted gross income instead of the total.

If you want to try to increase your financial aid package, make sure you do it in a tactful way. Ask the financial aid officer if you can "appeal" your offer. Don't use the term "negotiate," because it has a negative connotation. Explain that you really want to go to the school and you would really appreciate it if the school would consider adjusting your package.

Be honest and provide copies of the other offers you have received. Explain how much of an increase you need before you can enroll. You have nothing to lose by asking. Even though most financial aid officers do not want to get dragged into a bidding war, you should still request a better package with your first choice school. If you're a highly sought-after prospect, they will make every effort to meet your request.

Ask your guidance counselor to call the financial aid department and request the adjustment on your behalf. Most students who take this route find that their package increases. Also, if you win an outside scholarship, make sure to get the scholarship provider involved. Big companies who provide scholarships have a lot of clout with financial aid officers. If a school upsets a parent or student with its policy, it's just one student and one tuition at stake. But the school risks a wealth of future funding when they displease a prominent scholarship provider.

Watch Out For Scam Artists!

Watch out for "financial aid advisors" who offer their services for a fee and do any of the following things:

- Promise you a scholarship. (No one can guarantee you an award.)
- Say the "scholarships" they will help you find are not publicized. (Scholarships widely publicize their competitions because they want to choose the winner from a strong pool of applicants.)
- Offer to search a scholarship database for you. (Never pay for this service—it's free!)
- Pressure you to commit right away. (Avoid fast-talking salesmen.)
- Ask inappropriate questions about your finances or related information. (This is none of their business.)

- Request bank or credit card account number to "hold" a scholarship for you. (Never provide information.)
- Invite you to a free financial planning "seminar." When families arrive, they're hit with a high-pressure sales pitch for costly services that may include career counseling, rearranging assets to increase a family's calculated need for aid, and an "exclusive" scholarship search that, in reality, you could perform at little or no cost. (The services can run as much as $1,000 and offer little or nothing of worth-sometimes a basic skills assessment or canned financial advice.)
- Be sure to check out "Scholarship Scams" at www.ftc.gov

Tips for Getting the Most Aid

- Alert the aid office before you apply to irregularities regarding your parents' finances like an upcoming one-time bonus, pending hospital bills because of a serious illness, an inheritance, a business start-up or serious reversal. The more the office knows, the better.
- Beat the deadline and submit your application before it is due. Dealing with a family's tangled finances during crunch time puts tremendous pressure on over-worked aid representatives. That's when mistakes happen. Also, a lot of aid is awarded on a first-come, first-served basis.
- Get organized. Keep your files updated, know the facts, and maintain a call log to verify whom you've been talking with, when you talked to them, and the content of those conversations.
- Go to the top. If you're not satisfied with what you're hearing from an aid representative, ask politely but firmly to speak with the director of financial aid. Most directors say their phone lines are open to anyone who calls.
- Always answer financial aid applications honestly. If an aid officer ever notices a discrepancy between what you write on your application and your parents' tax returns, you will need to repay the money owed plus fines.

Financial Aid Horror Stories

Samantha - Los Angeles, CA
Samantha landed a role in a commercial and figured she could use the $8,000 paycheck to help with college. However, the college added the one time income to her assets and she lost over $3,200 in grant money because of it. She had to increase her student loans and go into debt. To avoid this happening to you keep focused on your grades to help with financial aid and be careful how much you work. A key fact to know is the federal government reduces aid by 50 cents for every dollar over $2,500 you earn. Even worse, they reduce aid by 85 cents for every dollar over $2,500 you have saved.

Louisa - Dallas, TX
Another example shows the importance of the deadline. When Louisa's family received financial aid forms in January they did not have all of the information they needed to fill them out (tax returns). Her father waited until March when he received the information and immediately sent out the forms. However, when Louisa received her aid award letter it was $10,000 less than then prior year. By the time the office received her forms all of the grant money was gone. Some tips to avoid this happening to you:
1. Take deadlines seriously
2. Send all forms in as soon as possible, there is no harm in them being early
3. If you do not yet have your tax return, there is a form FAFSA uses to estimate it until you receive it.

Legitimate Ways to Help Increase Your Aid Package

- Use savings to pay off credit cards, car loans, or other debt. These items are not figured into your family's net assets. The lower your family's assets and income, the more aid you will receive.
- Avoid taking large capital gains in the year used to determine aid. These gains count as both assets and income.
- Reduce assets in the student's name. Federal law requires that 35% of those assets must be defined as the student's share of first-year expenses, while the take is no more than about 5.6% of parents' assets (and roughly $40,000 is not counted).
- Notify the financial aid office in writing about anything unusual in your family's financial situation like a large medical expense.

Apply For Local Scholarships

Many corporations and non-profit organizations offer scholarship competitions. Your high school's guidance office probably keeps a list of scholarships, and it's smart to call organizations to see if they offer awards. Churches, Synagogues, 4-H Clubs, Rotary Clubs, Kiwanis Clubs, Lions Club, and Boys & Girls Clubs are all good places to start. The site www.FastWeb.com is also a great resource. Some of these scholarships may only amount to a few hundred dollars, but every little bit helps!

Write the Best Application Essays You Can

It will be well worth the effort. Ask your parents and teachers to critique your drafts. You can reuse the same essay for different applications, but make sure to personalize it for the specific award. Some important tips to write good essays:

- Be yourself
- Don't be gimmicky
- Think small (Most essays are 500 words which is not enough for a complex story)
- Don't wait until the last minute
- Don't let someone else write your essay (You could get caught and admissions counselors generally know how 17 and 18 year olds write)
- Revise and proofread twice

Low-Interest Rates on College Loans Available

If your family is like most others in the United States and is unable to completely afford college expenses, you can take out a low-interest loan. Remember, you don't need to borrow the amount needed for all four years. You just need enough to get you through one year at a time.

Tuition Payment Plans

For under $100 per year, Academic Management Services (508-235-2900), a financial service company can spread your tuition payments over 10 to 12 months, interest-free. This way you don't have to pay the entire first year bill in one lump sum. Many universities also offer an interest-free monthly payment plan.

Free Aid Information Available On-Line

Two of the best Web sites, say financial-aid experts, are FastWEB (www.fastweb.com) and US News & World Reports (www.usnews.com). Both feature comprehensive searchable databases of scholarships, so you can enter information such as age, gender, class rank, and track of study and receive a list of grants and loans that fit your profile.

Be Careful About How Much Money You Borrow

Last year, more than five million students borrowed a record $40 billion for college, three times the 1990 level. At some schools, graduates leave campus with an average debt of $30,000. To make matters worse, most undergraduates misjudge how much they're going to owe after they leave college, and how this debt might affect their future plans.

To avoid any surprises, visit an aid officer periodically during college, beginning in January of your freshman year,. Keep track of how fast the loans are piling up and get some help on how to build your loan repayment obligations into compensation you will receive when you enter the work force.

One way to stay abreast of your accumulating federal debt is by visiting the National Student Loan Data System (www.nslds.ed.gov)

Over 4,000 scholarship opportunities

Go to www.FreeScholarshipGuide.com for a complete list. Here is a small sample:

Scholarship	Value	Link
AICPA Scholarships	Up to $5,000	www.aicpa.org
Barry M. Goldwater Scholarship	Up to $7,500	www.act.org/goldwater
Burger King Scholars Program	$1,000	www.bkscholars.csfa.org
Collegenet Scholarship	Up to $15,000	www.collegenet.com
Elks National Foundation	$1,000 to $15,000 per year	www.elks.org/enf/scholars
Japanese American Citizens League	30 from $1,000-$5,000	www.jacl.org
John F. Kennedy "Profile in Courage"	$500-$3,000	www.jfkcontest.org
Got milk? SAMMY Awards	25 scholarships of $7,500	www.whymilk.com/index.htm
MBNA Foundation Award	$1,000 to $7,500	www.mbnafoundation.org
The Ron Brown Scholar Program	$40,000	www.ronbrown.org
Robert C. Byrd Honors Scholarship	$4,000 to $6,000	www.ed.gov
Tylenol Scholarship	10 $10,000, 150 $1,000	www.scholarship.tylenol.com
U.S. Bank's Internet Scholarship Program	Up to 30 $1,000	www.usbank.com/studentloans

10 Tips from a Scholarship Judge

1)   Use the scholarship application. Don't retype the question. One applicant thought she was being thorough by typing out each question on another sheet, with her answer underneath it. But, judges go through a lot of applications, and they get used to seeing information in the same place. A typed-out application is harder to read. Plus, this particular applicant left off one of the questions, and knocked her out of the running.

2)   Fill out the practice application first. Photocopy the application and use the copy to write a draft. Once you've fine-tuned your answers, type them neatly on the original.

3)   Pay attention to detail. Most applications ask for your name, address, date of birth, and expected graduation date. Be careful. Omitting information can cost you. The applications I read asked students under 18 to have a parent sign the form. Applicants who ignored that had a mark against them from the start.

4)   Be concise, but creative. What you write, not how much you write, will impress judges. Emphasize what makes you different from everybody else. Let your personality show through so judges can feel connected to you.

5)   Have self-respect. When explaining how you overcame hardship, do not over state your difficulties. The judge should admire you and you achievements, not squirm in her seat.

6)   Be humble. When reporting accomplishments, be humble. Try to convey your dedication and skill, but also maintain modesty. Watch for a bragging tone.

7)   Do the math. If an application asks for your family's income or college expenses, make sure those financial numbers are correct.

8)   Choose your teachers wisely. Often, it's hard to pick scholarship winners from a pool of so many excellent entries. Outstanding teacher letters may make the difference.

9)   Help your teachers write the best letters. Give them a summary of your achievements and goals and all the scholarship information.

10) Do not miss the deadline. After you work hard putting together the best possible application, make sure it will be read!

FINISH LINE: Sadly, there are a lot of families who mistakenly believe that their child's tuition will be fully paid-for when they receive an athletic scholarship. Too often, these families get a rude awakening when their child either doesn't get a full ride, or doesn't get a scholarship at all.

Now's the time to take an honest look at your family's financial situation and begin to look at your options for paying for college. Here are some steps to follow:

*   Use FastWeb or another service to identify some potential scholarships.
*   Contact local companies/organizations and your school's guidance department to identify local scholarship opportunities.
*   Apply for as many scholarships as you can.
*   Explore loans and other means of getting aid.
*   Work on your application essays.

FINANCIAL AID TIMELINE

November:
- If you are applying for early decision, remember that most schools have deadlines in mid-November.
- Check if any high schools in the area offer free workshops on how to complete financial aid forms.

December:
- Complete your FAFSA, but do not mail it until January. Make sure you have properly signed and dated the document. Any mistakes can delay the process and result in lost financial aid.
- Keep copies of everything you mail.

January:
- To qualify for the most aid possible, submit your FAFSA as early as you can after January.
- If you sent your FAFSA on January or shortly after that, you should receive a Student Aid Report (SAR) indicating your eligibility for aid and your family's expected contribution.
- Make any corrections to your SAR, including updates based on your family's federal 1040 tax form
- Sign, date, and return the SAR to the address designated.

March:
- Receive a corrected SAR if needed
- Make sure a copy of the corrected SAR reaches the financial aid office at each college you are applying to.

April:
- You may receive notices of admission and financial aid awards. You can begin to compare offers.

May:
- May 1 is the traditional Candidate's Reply Date. You must accept an offer from one school and decline all others.
- Complete any loan forms.

June & July:
- Consider working during the summer so you will have money for expenses when you arrive on campus.
- Continue to explore scholarships. You will need funds beyond freshman year and new scholarships appear every year. Make note of which of your scholarships are renewable.

SERVE YOUR COUNTRY & GET A GREAT EDUCATION!

Army: U.S. Military Academy, NY

Division - ROTC
What You Get: Full scholarship (tuition, books, fees); stipend up to $400/month while in school
What You Give: 4 years of active duty; 4 years reserve duty; 1 ROTC class per semester; weekly drills
To Qualify: SAT 920; ACT 19; Age 17–21
Info: 800-USA-ROTC; www.goarmy.com

Division - Active GI Bill
What You Get: Up to $32,400 for college after discharge; with Army College Fund up to $50,000 in some military job areas; student loan repayment up to $65,000; 75% tuition assistance during service
What You Give: At least 2 years of active duty; $1,200 contribution over course of one year toward benefit
To Qualify: H.S. diploma or equivalent; Age 17–35
Info: 800-USA-ARMY; www.goarmy.com

Division - Reserve GI Bill
What You Get: $9,936 for college after discharge; loan repayment up to $20,000
What You Give: 1 weekend/ month; 2 weeks/year for 6 years
To Qualify: H.S. diploma or equivalent; age 17–35
Info: 800-USA-ARMY; www.goarmy.com

Division - Guard GI Bill
What You Get: Up to $9,936 over 36 months; 75% tuition assistance; all states offer additional tuition assistance programs
What You Give: 3–6 years enlistment; 1 weekend/month; 2 weeks/year
To Qualify: H.S diploma or equivalent
Info: 800-GO-GUARD

NAVY: U.S. Naval Academy, Annapolis, MD

Division - ROTC
What You Get: Full scholarship (tuition, books, fees); stipend up to $400/month while in school
What You Give: 3 years active duty; 5 years reserve duty
To Qualify: SAT 1050; ACT 22
Info: 800-NAV-ROTC; www.nrotc.navy.mil

Division - Active GI Bill
What You Get: Up to $28,800; with Navy College Fund up to $15,000 in some jobs; 75% tuition assistance up to $3,500/year; seaman-to-admiral (STA), $10,000; tuition repayment up to $10,000
What You Give: 2-6 years active duty; $1,200 contribution (STA: 5 years active duty upon commissioning)
To Qualify: H.S diploma or equivalent (STA: SAT 1000; ACT 21) Age 18–34
Info: 800-USA-NAVY; www.navyjobs.com

Division - Reserve GI Bill
What You Get: $9,936 for college after discharge; loan repayment up to $20,000
What You Give: 1 weekend/month; 2 weeks/year; 4–6 years active duty
To Qualify: H.S. diploma or equivalent; Age 21–38
Info: 866-NAVRES1; www.navalreserve.com

MARINES

Division - ROTC
What You Get: Full scholarship (tuition, books, fees); stipend $200/month while in school

What You Give: 4–6 years active duty
To Qualify: SAT 1050; ACT 22
Info: 800-USA-NAVY; www.nrotc.navy.mil

Division - Active GI Bill
What You Get: Up to $28,000 after discharge; 100% tuition assistance
What You Give: 3–5 years active duty; $1,200 contribution
To Qualify: H.S. diploma or equivalent
Info: 800-MARINES; www.marines.com

Division - Reserve GI Bill
What You Get: $7,124.40 for college after discharge
What You Give: 1 weekend/month; 2 weeks/year for 6 years
To Qualify: H.S. diploma or equivalent
Info: 800-MARINES; www.marines.com

AIR FORCE - U.S. Air Force Academy, Colorado Springs, CO

Division - ROTC
What You Get: Full scholarship; books up to $510/year; stipend up to $400/month
What You Give: 4 years active duty
To Qualify: SAT 1100; ACT 24
Info: 866-4AFROTC; www.afrotc.com

Division - Active GI Bill
What You Get: Up to $40,000 after discharge; college credit for training; 100% tuition assistance up to $4,500/year; loan repayment up to $10,000
What You Give: 4–6 years active duty; $1,200 contribution plus; $600 to increase benefit by $5,400
To Qualify: H.S. diploma or equivalent
Info: 800-423-USAF; www.airforce.com

Division - Reserve GI Bill
What You Get: Up to $9,936; more for some jobs; 100% tuition assistance up to $4,500/year during service
What You Give: 1 weekend/month; 2 weeks/year for 6 years
To Qualify: H.S. diploma or equivalent
Info: 800-257-1212; www.afreserve.com

Division - Selected Reserve Guard GI Bill
What You Get: Up to $9,036; state National Guard units offer additional tuition assistance and loan repayment benefits
What You Give: 3–6 years enlistment; 1 weekend/month; 2 weeks/year
To Qualify: H.S. diploma or equivalent
Info: 800-TO-GO-ANG; www.af.mil
Coast Guard: U.S. Coast Guard, New London, CT

Division - ROTC - No ROTC; College Student Pre-Commissioning Program for qualifying minority students
What You Get: $1,200/month during last two years
What You Give: 3 years active duty
To Qualify: SAT I 1000; SAT II 1100; ACT 21; GPA 2.5
Info: 877-NOW-USCG; www.gocoastguard.com

Division - Active GI Bill
What You Get: Up to $28,000
What You Give: 4-6 years active duty; 2-4 years reserve duty; $1,200 contribution
To Qualify: H.S. diploma or equivalent
Info: 877-NOW-USCG; www.gocoastguard.com

Division - Reserve GI Bill
What You Get: $9,936 for college after discharge; loan repayment up to $20,000
What You Give: 1 weekend/month; 2 weeks/year for 4 years
To Qualify: H.S. diploma or equivalent
Info: 800-424-8883; www.uscg.mil

Check each site you are interested in confirm all information.

Military Stories

"Through the Guard, I served one weekend a month and trained two weeks a year, and they paid 100% of my tuition for my degree in criminal justice. You have to be prepared to serve overseas. I worked with the military police in Uzbekistan. I hope to eventually work for local or state police."
–Jarred Tiberi, Sergeant, Military Police, U.S. Army National Guard, Melrose, MA

"I have been in the Army almost three years, and I have completed about 15 credit hours. I am currently taking two more classes toward my associate degree in criminal justice, and the Army gives 100 percent tuition assistance. One of the best programs is the EARMYU, which allows me to continue college study online."
–Ronzale C. Piersey, Sergeant U.S. Army, Fort Knox, KY

"In high school, I joined Navy ROTC, and after graduation, I joined the Marines. I took a military 'skills' test that told me I was suited for personnel administration, which is what I wanted to do. I plan on getting a degree in business administration taking advantage of tuition assistance.
–Veronica Robledo, Lance Corporal, Personnel Administration, U.S. Marines, Quantico, VA

CHAPTER 7

THE COLLEGE LANDSCAPE BY DIVISION

In This Chapter

- ◆ NCAA Division I
- ◆ NCAA Division II
- ◆ NCAA Division III
- ◆ NAIA
- ◆ NJCAA Division I
- ◆ NJCAA Division II
- ◆ NJCAA Division III

Now, it's time to get a clear picture of just how many options you truly have. This chapter details the eligibility requirements for each of the divisions.

NATIONAL COLLEGIATE ATHLETIC ASSOCIATION (NCAA)

The NCAA is the most powerful governing body for college sports. It represents three separate divisions (I, II, and III) featuring roughly 1,024 four-year schools.

Contact Info

NCAA
700 W. Washington St.
P.O. Box 6222
Indianapolis, IN 46206-6222
Web: www.ncaa.org
Phone: 317-917-6222
Fax: 317-917-6888
Publications: 888-388-9748

NCAA Clearinghouse

P.O. Box 4044
Iowa City, IA 52243-4044
Phone: 319-337-1492 or 888-388-9748
Fax: 319-337-1556
To check the status of your filing: 319-339-3003

You must register with the NCAA Clearinghouse after your junior year if you want to be considered an eligible recruit. This lets colleges know that you have met all their academic requirements.

To register, call **888-388-9748** to receive your free copy of the *NCAA Guide for the college-Bound Student Athlete.* This guide provides detailed information about the NCAA's requirements and contains a Student Release Form.

Mail or fax the white copy of the form to the Clearinghouse with the registration fee. Give the yellow and pink copies of the form to your guidance counselor who will send the yellow copy along with your transcript to the Clearinghouse. The Clearinghouse will send your eligibility status to any NCAA D-I or D-II school that requests it.

It is also very helpful to keep track of your eligibility yourself. Instead of only relying on your high school guidance counselor, keep track of your own eligibility status by checking that you are taking all of the required classes and are maintaining an acceptable GPA.

Many websites will help you do this. One good site is www.Prep48.com, which will prevent you from making a mistake and costing yourself years of eligibility. The website is free so login and track your progress throughout high school.

NCAA DIVISION I

NCAA DIVISION I

NCAA DIVISION I

D-I schools are mostly comprised of big schools that attract considerable media attention. They have the largest athletic budgets and recruit athletes nationally. They are the most popular with high school students because of their high-profile status. There are roughly 326 D-I schools in the country. (117 I-A, 121 I-AA, 88 I-AAA)

Academic Eligibility Requirements - Division I

Depending on your three criteria — GPA, SAT/ACT exam scores, and core courses — you will either be classified as a "Qualifier," "Partial Qualifier," or "Non Qualifier." Here are the requirements for each:

Qualifier Requirements

- Graduate High School
- Graduate with a core-course GPA and total SAT/ACT scores based on the Qualifier Index below.
- Successfully complete a core curriculum of at least 13 academic course units as follows:
- 4 years of English
- 2 years of Math
- 2 years of Social Science
- 2 years of Natural or Physical Science (including one lab class)
- 1 additional year in English, Math, or Natural or Physical Science.
- 2 more year of any of the above or Foreign Language, Computer Science, Philosophy, or Religion

Qualifier Index

Core GPA	ACT	SAT
2.5 & Above	68	820
2.475	70	830
2.450	70	840-850
2.425	70	860
2.400	71	860
2.375	72	870
2.350	73	880
2.325	74	890
2.300	75	900
2.275	76	910
2.250	77	920
2.225	78	930
2.200	79	940
2.175	80	950
2.150	80	960
2.125	81	960
2.100	82	970
2.075	83	980
2.050	84	990
2.025	85	1000
2.000	86	1010

Partial Qualifier Requirements

- ◆ Graduate High School
- ◆ Graduate with a core-course GPA and total SAT/ACT scores based on the Index below
- ◆ Successfully complete a core curriculum of at least 13 academic course units (same courses as "Qualifier Requirements")

If you are a Partial Qualifier, you cannot play in games during your first year at a Division I school, but you can practice with the team at the home facility and receive a scholarship. You will have three seasons left of eligibility. You can earn a fourth year of eligibility if you receive a bachelor's degree before the start of your fifth year of college.

Partial Qualifier Index

Core GPA	ACT	SAT
2.750 & Above	59	720
2.725	59	730
2.700	60	730
2.2.675	61	740-750
2.650	62	760
2.625	63	770
2.600	64	780
2.575	65	790
2.550	66	800
2.525	67	810

Non-Qualifier

You will be classified as a Non-Qualifier if you fail to graduate from high school or do not meet the core-curriculum GPA and SAT/ACT scores required for a Qualifier.

If you are a Non-Qualifier, you cannot practice with the team, play games, or receive a scholarship during your first year. You will have three seasons left of eligibility. You can earn a fourth year of eligibility if you receive a bachelor degree before the start of your fifth year of college.

Division I

If you enroll in a Division I college and want to participate in athletics or receive an athletics scholarship during your first year, you must:

- ◆ Graduate from high school;
- ◆ Complete these 16 core courses:
- ◆ 4 years of English
- ◆ 3 years of math (algebra 1 or higher)
- ◆ 2 years of natural or physical science (including one year of lab science if offered)
- ◆ 1 extra year of English, math or natural or physical science
- ◆ 2 years of social science
- ◆ 4 years of extra core courses (from any category above, foreign language, religion or philosophy)
- ◆ Earn a minimum required GPA in your core courses
- ◆ Earn a combined SAT or ACT sum score that matches your core-course GPA and test score

Computer science courses can be used as core courses only if your high school grants graduation credit in math or natural or physical science for them, and if the courses appear on your high school's core course list as a math or science course.

What are Core Courses?

See your high school's core course list at www.ncaaclearinghouse.net.

NCAA DIVISION II

D-II schools are medium-sized schools and recruit on a smaller scale and have fewer scholarship opportunities than D-I schools. There are roughly 279 D-II schools.

Academic Eligibility Requirements - Division II

Depending on your three criteria — GPA, SAT/ACT exam scores, and core courses — you will either be classified as a Qualifier, Partial Qualifier, or Non Qualifier. Here are the requirements for each:

Qualifier Requirements

- Graduate High School
- Graduate with a 2.0 core course GPA
- Score a minimum combined SAT score
- Successfully complete a core curriculum of at least 13 academic course units as follows:
  - 3 years of English
  - 2 years of Math
  - 2 years of Social Science
  - 2 years of Natural or Physical Science (including one lab class)
  - 2 additional years of English, Math, or Natural or Physical Science
  - 2 more years of any of the above or Foreign Language, Computer Science, Philosophy, or religion

Partial Qualifier

- Graduate High School
- Score a minimum combined SAT score, or…
- Graduate with a 2.0 core-course GPA and successfully complete a core curriculum of at least 13 academic courses (same as "Qualifier Requirements")

If you are a Partial Qualifier, you cannot play in games during your first year, but you can practice with the team at the home facility and receive a scholarship. You will have four seasons left of eligibility.

Non-Qualifier Requirements

You will be classified as a Non Qualifier if you fail to graduate from high school or do not meet the core-curriculum GPA and SAT/ACT scores required for a qualifier. If you are a Non-Qualifier, you cannot practice with the team, play games, or receive a scholarship during your first year. You will have four seasons left of eligibility.

Division II

2005 and Later

If you enroll in a Division II college and want to participate in athletics or receive an athletics scholarship during your first year, you must:

- Graduate from high school,
- Complete these 14 core courses:
    - 3 years of English
    - 2 years of math (algebra 1 or higher)
    - 2 years of natural or physical science (including one year of lab science if offered)
    - 2 extra years of English, math or natural or physical science
    - 2 years of social science
    - 3 years of extra core courses (from above, or foreign language, non-doctrinal religion or philosophy);
- Earn a 2.0 GPA or better in your core courses; and
- Earn a minimum combined SAT

There is no sliding scale in Division II.

Computer science courses can be used as core courses only if your high school grants graduation credit in math or natural or physical science for them, and if the courses appear on your high school's core-course list as a math or science course.

NCAA DIVISION III

D-III schools tend to recruit regionally, do not offer scholarships, but comprise some of the most prestigious academic schools in the country. There are roughly 419 D-III schools and none offer scholarships, though many offer generous academic scholarships.

Academic Eligibility Requirements

D-III schools do not have standard requirements. Check with the individual schools that interest you for details.

NATIONAL ASSOCIATION OF INTERCOLLEGIATE ATHLETICS (NAIA)

The NAIA represents roughly 288 four-year schools. The NAIA is separate from the NCAA and began in 1937. The organization is divided into thirty-two districts representing the 50 states, and it sponsors district and national championships in a variety of sports. Similar to the NCAA, the NAIA awards full or partial scholarships if students meet eligibility requirements.

Contact Info

NAIA
23500 W. 105th St.
P.O. Box 1325
Olathe, KS 66051
Web: www.naia.org
Phone: 913-791-0044

Academic Eligibility Requirements

You must meet two of the following three eligibility requirements:

- Graduate in the upper half of your high school class
- Earn a minimum combined score
- Earn a 2.0 cumulative GPA

For a complete list of eligibility requirements, procedures, guidelines, and association by-laws, call the NAIA and ask to receive a copy of their manual, *A Guide for the College-Bound Athlete.*

NATIONAL JUNIOR COLLEGE ATHLETIC ASSOCIATION (NJCAA)

The NJCAA consists of roughly 503 two-year programs representing three separate divisions (I, II, and III). D-I and D-II schools offer up to 24 scholarships, depending on the sport. D-III schools do not offer scholarships.

The NJCAA has member schools in 42 states, and is the national governing body of 15 men's and 12 women's sports over three divisions. Approximately 45,300 athletes compete in one of 24 regions and every year the NJCAA hosts 48 national championships.

If you yearn for the experience of living in a dorm, spending Saturday afternoons cheering for the home football team, and enjoying an active social life, you should choose a four-year school. If not, a junior college may be a perfect option for you. While most JCs offer a wide array of extracurricular activities, the students commute and many of them work full-time, so they have less time for social activities.

You have two options if you attend a JC. The first is called a Transfer Program, which enables you to leave school after one or two years and transfer your credits earned to a four-year school. The second option is called a Terminal Program, which earns you an associate's degree after attending school for two years.

Contact Info
NJCAA
1755 Telstar Dr.
Colorado Springs, CO 809920
Phone: 719-590-9788
Web: www.njcaa.org

Academic Requirements
JCs generally offer an open-door admission policy so you don't have to worry about getting in; however, you must meet one of the following requirements:

- Graduate from high school
- Receive a high school equivalency diploma
- Pass a national test such as the General Education Development Test (GED)

For a complete list of eligibility requirements, procedures, guidelines, and association by-laws, call the NJCAA and ask to receive a copy of their manual, *NJCAA Handbook & Casebook*.

Letter Of Intent
The NJCAA Letter of Intent is used to commit an individual to a specific institution for a period of one year and is only valid for NJCAA colleges. You may sign a Letter of Intent with both a NJCAA college and a NCAA college, but may not sign a Letter of Intent with two NJCAA colleges. If you sign a Letter of Intent with two NJCAA colleges, you will be ineligible for one year.

Benefits of Attending a Junior College

Attending a JC is a great option for many athletes. Here are some reasons why you may want to consider this route:

Your GPA, SAT/ACT, or Core Courses Did Not Meet the Four-Year Schools' Requirements

If you did not apply yourself academically in high school and your marks are not indicative of your full potential, you might be better off starting college with a year or two of JC and then transferring to a four-year school.

You Need another Year At Home Before Going Away To School

If you feel that another year living at home would help ease the transition to a four-year college, then a local JC is a good option.

You Don't Want To Compete At Any Of The Four-Year Schools To Which You've been Accepted

If you got a late start preparing for college and are not happy with the schools you've been admitted to, a year of JC exposure may give you a better opportunity to fully explore all your four-year options.

Your Family Cannot Afford To Send You to a Four-Year School at This Time

Tuition at JCs is very affordable and athletic scholarships are more plentiful. Even if you don't receive a scholarship, you can attend most for only a couple of thousand dollars a year.

You Also Want To Work Full-Time

A JC is also a practical choice for students who need class schedules flexible enough to accommodate full-time jobs. The schools typically offer classes from 8 a.m. to 10 p.m. weekdays and on Saturday mornings to accommodate students with jobs.

FINISH LINE: Take some time to go through the requirements at each of the levels to see where you fit. If you haven't already, register with the NCAA Clearinghouse. You should also use the online directory to locate some schools you might have previously overlooked in building your Target List.

WEB SITES BY SPORT

Baseball
www.abca.org: American Baseball Coaches Association
www.Baseball-links.com: Baseball related links
www.Hsbaseballweb.com: High school baseball news, links, showcases
www.Aaronslinks.com: Baseball related links
www.Heavyhitter.com: Baseball related links
www.Thebaseballportal.com: Baseball related links

Basketball
www.wbca.org: Women's Basketball Coaches Association
www.Thebasketballportal.com: Basketball related links
www.Basketball-toplinks.com: All basketball related links
www.collegehoopsnet.com: College news, basketball links, recruiting info
www.Rivalshoops.com: College basketball recruiting news and links
www.Hoopmasters.com: College basketball recruiting news
www.D3hoops.com: Division III news and info

Field Hockey
www.nfhca.org: National Field Hockey Coaches Association
www.Usfieldhockey.com: Official site of USA field hockey
www.Hockeylinx.com: Hockey related links
www.Planetfieldhockey.com: International news, coaching & training tips

Football
www.afca.org: American Football Coaches Association
www.Ncaafootball.net: News and results for all divisions
www.Thefootballportal.com: Football related links
www.Football-links.com: Football related links
www.Nflhs.com: NFL high school news, tips, and drills

Golf
www.ngca.com/index.jsp: National Golf Coaches Association
www.Cgfgolf.org: College Golf Foundation
www.Nagce.org: National Association for Golf Coaches & Educators

Ice Hockey
www.ahcahockey.com: American Hockey Coaches Association
www.brown.edu/Athletics/Womens_Hockey/AWHCA/: American Women's Hockey Coaches Association
www.collegehockey.org: College, prep, junior, & pro news, links, camps
www.Azhockey.com: Links, news, stats
www.Uscollegehockey.com : College stats, standings, news, polls
www.Hockeydb.com: Internet database, stats, leagues, message boards
www.Thehockeyportal.com: Hockey related links

Lacrosse
www.lacrosse.org: US Lacrosse
www.iwlca.org: Intercollegiate Women's Lacrosse Coaches Association
www.Laxlinks.com: Lacrosse related links
www.Youthlacrosseusa.com: News, ranking, recruiting, rules, tips, camps
www.Insidelacrosse.com: High school, college, & pro news, recruiting info
www.Alllacrosseamerica.com: Links, news, message boards, camps
www.Laxtips.com: Text and audio tips from pro and college players

Skiing
www.Usskiteam.com: United States Ski Team
www.Skinet.com: News, links, merchandise

Soccer
www.nscaa.com: National Soccer Coaches Association of America
www.Soccer-corner.com: Soccer related links
www.Thesoccerportal.com: Soccer related links
www.Soccer-toplinks.com: Soccer related links
www.Soccerinfo.com: Camps, tournaments, & recruiting info

Softball
www.nfcaa.org: National Fast Pitch Coaches Association
www.Softballtournaments.com: Tournament listing, links, forums
www.Playnsa.com: National Softball Association
www.Softball.org: Amateur Softball Association of America

Swimming
www.swimmingcoach.org: American Swimming Coaches Association
www.Cscaa.org: College Swimming Coaches Association of America
www.Nisca.net: National Interscholastic Swimming Coaches Association
www.Swimnews.com: News, results, forums, links

Tennis
www.ushsta.org: United States High School Tennis Association
www.Thetennisportal.com: Tennis related links
www.collegetennisonline.com: News, rankings, links to camps
www.collegeandjuniortennis.com: News, rankings, schedules
www.Itatennis.com: Intercollegiate Tennis Association
www.Tennisserver.com: News, links, rules, organizations, tips
www.Tennis4all.com: Links, info, message boards, organizations

Track/Cross Country
www.runmichigan.com/links/list/org.1037993130.19797.html: United States Track Coaches Association
www.usccca.org: United States Cross Country Coaches Association
www.Dyestat.com: High school track portal
www.Track-and-field.net: Links, stats, news, track merchandise
www.Tflinks.com: Track and field links

www.Usatf.org: Links merchandise, rules
www.Trackinfo.org: Links, events

Volleyball
www.avca.org: American Volleyball Coaches Association
www.Volleyball.com: Forums, coaches corner, links
www.Volleyball.org: International high school, college, & pro news
www.Cvu.com: Collegiate scores, standings, news, links
www.Usavolleyball.org: News, events, camps, rules

Wrestling
www.nwcaonline.com: National Wrestling Coaches Association
www.Ncwa.net: National Collegiate Wrestling Association
www.Themat.com: Camps, links, news, rankings, results
www.Intermatwrestle.com: News, results, links, camps, forums
www.Amateurwrestler.com: Forums, training and health tips

FINISH LINE: Take some time to go through the requirements at each of the levels to see where you fit. If you haven't already, register with the NCAA Clearinghouse. You can also use the division lists by sport on the following pages to locate some schools you might have previously overlooked in building your Target List.

COLLEGE CLUB TEAMS

Rise of Club Teams Creates a Whole New Level of Success
By BILL PENNINGTON in the *New York Times*

In intercollegiate club sports, there are no athletic scholarships, no adoring crowds and minimal adult leadership. Institutional financing is meager and hard work abundant, with dozens of volunteer hours required from the athletes just to put on a single game or match.

It's college athletics without the pageantry or prerogative, and that's the way athletes in club sports like it. They devise the practices, make the team rules, decide whom to play and when, raise the money for uniforms and game officials, schedule the hotel and travel arrangements and manage the paperwork.

"It's a ton of work, but we do it because we take ownership of our team," said David Gerstle, the player-coach of Yale's club water polo team, which like most club teams operates largely outside the purview of the university athletic department. "I think it's a more collegial experience than the varsity team model."

College club sports are swiftly rising in popularity, a largely unnoticed phenomenon sweeping across campuses nationwide. These are not intramural sports but expertly organized, highly skilled teams that often belong to regional conferences and play for national collegiate championships. Twenty years ago the national club volleyball championship drew 20 teams and 206 male athletes. Last spring, the same championship hosted 258 teams and 2,806 participants in four men's divisions and two women's divisions.

The soccer club championship started in 1994 by the National Intramural-Recreational Sports Association had 15 teams and 252 male and female players. Last year, it had 75 teams and 1,380 players. The inaugural tennis tournament in 2000 drew 11 teams and 89 participants. In 2008, it had grown to 64 teams and 523 participants, with 20 teams on a waiting list.

An estimated two million college students play competitive club sports compared with about 430,000 involved in athletics governed by the National Collegiate Athletic Association and the National Association of Intercollegiate Athletics.

The less restrictive nature of club teams has also been a magnet for the thriving nontraditional sports market. While many NCAA athletic departments are cutting varsity sports, club teams are competing for national championships in bass fishing, ballroom dancing and Brazilian martial arts. Because of this independent and inclusive spirit, competitive club sports have emerged as an alternative to the semiprofessional, regulated, commercial environment of modern, elite college athletics.

"It is a return to pure amateurism and a lot closer to the original model for college athletics," said Jim Giunta, the executive director of the National Collegiate Wrestling Association, which hosted 70 club teams at its most recent national championships, an increase from 17 teams 10 years ago.

"Nobody competes for the money or the fame because there are no scholarships and not a lot of attention. The kids have to do all the work to make their club function. They do it because they love their sport, and I'll tell you what, we don't have the prima donnas you see at the higher levels of college athletics."

Several other factors are driving the club sports boom. One frequently mentioned by college officials is America's outsize youth sports culture. With more than 40 million children playing organized sports — often on first-rate travel teams — more students are graduating from high school with extensive athletic interest and skills than ever before.

A small number of those graduates, fewer than 5 percent, are good enough to play a varsity college sport. That leaves many thousands who are accustomed to competing at a high level and looking for an athletic outlet.

"Intramural sports can be too loose and not competitive enough," said Tiffany Villalba, a senior on Villanova University's women's club soccer team, which won the open division at the national championships last season. "But the varsity teams, even if you make one, can be intense and require a lot of your free time. The club team fills that big gap between the two. It's not too demanding, but it's not trivial."

The ability to balance one's academic, athletic and social life is an apparent draw to the club sports model. Chip Spear, a volunteer coach for the Yale water polo team, said that one of his players was a member of the Whiffenpoofs, Yale's celebrated a cappella group.

"He misses some practices for their engagements," said Spear, who played water polo at Yale when it was still a varsity sport. "The team works it out because all practices are not mandatory. I'm not sure how that would have worked on a varsity team." Students say they sometimes choose a club sport (like sailing) for cultural or lifestyle reasons or because it was not available in high school (like Ultimate Frisbee).

In either case, the students shape and influence the makeup and philosophy of the team, and tailor their commitment to it. College administrators said they put club sports in the same category as student development.

"Being active in the leadership of a club sport teaches a wealth of real-life lessons that college students might not learn anywhere else," said Chris McAlpine, who coordinates recreation and club sports at Villanova. "What they are doing is résumé building, like an internship. I get a lot of business reference calls, and I'll be asked: 'Did so-and-so work well with others? Can she follow through on a project?'

"And I'll answer: 'Well, she led a team of 25 girls, balanced a $12,000 budget, handled travel arrangements in 5 states and planned 100 practices. Oh, her team won, too.' " With no single national governing body for all club sports, teams operate differently from institution to institution. Most are overseen by a student activities association, which doles out money to individual clubs that apply with their financial requests. Some clubs may get $500, some $20,000, if they make an exceptionally good case for needing the money.

Typical university financing is a few thousand dollars. At that point, the clubs solicit sponsorships from the community and seek donations from alumni who played the sport. Almost all teams require players to pay an annual fee, which can range from $50 to more than $1,000 for an expensive sport like ice hockey. Fund-raising car washes and raffles are common. Getting players to pitch in to help is not usually a problem. Club sports have become so popular that many teams have tryouts, cuts and waiting lists.

Each sport generally has a national governing body, which often helps with scheduling and rule uniformity and hosts a championship tournament. In many cases, that governing body will require that all the athletes attending the nationals have at least a 2.0 grade point average.

The interaction between club and varsity athletes is limited, but the two sectors generally work together amiably. Fields, courts and pools usually have to be shared, although the varsity programs always take priority.

Occasional friction develops when a handful of varsity athletes quit to play on a club team, but a majority of varsity athletic administrators expressed support of the mission of club sports.

"I see only positives in an outlet that lets college students keep competing in a sport," said Tim Selgo, the athletic director at Grand Valley State University in Allendale, Mich., whose club wrestling team has won the past three national championships. "There are always conflicts over scheduling of facilities, but no college has enough room. Hey, our club women's rugby team beat Michigan State last month. That's a source of great pride; it made everybody feel good."

Club athletes interviewed conceded that they were occasionally envious of the varsity players, who not only have status on campus but may receive scholarships, dress in lavish locker rooms and travel in luxury.

"It's easy to be jealous when you're watching the varsity kids board a nice coach bus as someone loads their equipment for them," said Betsy Pantazelos, a recent captain of Boston University's club ski racing team. "We would be standing there waiting for our little van, which we would jam full with kids and all our equipment and then take turns driving. The frustration would build when it broke down on the side of the road and we had no one to help us.

"But you can learn a lot from those situations, like arranging for emergency road service. There was always an attitude that we can get through this and find a way to do it better next time."

Pure Enjoyment

The entrepreneurial spirit of the modern college student is a factor often cited when explaining the growth of club sports on campuses. The Internet receives its share of credit too.

"With the new technologies, they are savvier and communicate far better: e-mail, Facebook, all that," said Andy Lewandowski, another former Yale varsity water polo player who is a volunteer coach. "They can rally support for a cause in a flash. New club sports teams sprout up on this campus every semester."

Clubs have been so enjoyable for many college students that if given the chance to turn their teams into fully financed varsity sports, most said they would decline.

"It would be less fun," Jacob Tulipan, a Yale senior who plays water polo, said. "We wouldn't be doing it for the same reasons."

Gerstle, Tulipan's teammate, explained why he preferred the club model.

"If you look at it in economic terms, varsity sports are like a high-regulated industry with restrictions, caps and incentives," Gerstle said as he stood next to the pool before a recent practice. "But club sports eliminate the barriers and let anyone in, much like libertarian economics. It raises the level of competition because it inspires people's competitive nature. It frees them to want to do it and do their best."

Preparing to jump into the pool, Gerstle, a physics major, added, "It's also sport for the love of sport."

CHAPTER 8

FORMS YOU'LL NEED AND REFERENCES YOU'LL USE

In This Chapter

- Checklists to guide you through each year of high school
- Sample correspondence and profile
- Useful web sites
- Form to help you identify your top school
- Charts for figuring costs and your family contribution

This chapter serves as a catch-all for the topics that were covered earlier in the Guide. Here you'll find useful tools to help you through the confusing recruiting process.

CHECKLIST

FRESHMEN SCHOOL YEAR & SUMMER

Academic

- ☐ Take the most challenging courses you can handle.

- ☐ Prioritize your classes, putting the core ones at the top.

- ☐ Meet your guidance counselor and let her know of your desire to compete in college. Make sure they know that you must meet the core course requirement.

- ☐ Find a tutor, create a study group, and become comfortable interacting with teachers outside of class for extra help.

- ☐ Work hard at school and strive for a 4.0 GPA.

- ☐ Learn to manage your time and develop good study habits.

- ☐ Visit any college campuses you can. The best choices are your parents' alma maters and the schools of relatives, siblings, and friends currently attending college.

Athletics

- ☐ Attend a game or match at your nearest college.

- ☐ Purchase instructional tapes to help you improve your skills.

- ☐ Start a weight lifting program (ask your trainer for advice).

- ☐ Stay in shape year round.

- ☐ Compete for your high school team.

- ☐ Compete for off-season club teams.

- ☐ Attend a summer camp.

SOPHOMORE SCHOOL YEAR & SUMMER

Academic

- ☐ Make a commitment to improve your grades and take challenging courses.

- ☐ Meet with your guidance counselor to make sure you are taking classes to satisfy your core course requirement and staying on track. Discuss the possibility of AP classes for junior year

- ☐ Hire a tutor, form a study group with your friends, and seek extra help from your teachers in order to improve your GPA.

- ☐ Start researching various careers in which you might have interest to give you an idea of potential college majors.

☐   Make a preliminary Target List. Include as many schools as possible.

☐   Take the PSAT so you know where you need to improve.

☐   Visit more college campuses.

Athletics

☐   Make unofficial visits to as many schools on your Target List as possible.

☐   Stay in shape year round by running and lifting weights

☐   Compete on your high school team.

☐   Compete for off-season club teams.

☐   Attend an off-season sports camp.

☐   Research showcases or tournaments and attend at least one.

JUNIOR SCHOOL YEAR & SUMMER
Academic

☐   Make a commitment to improve your grades and take challenging courses.

☐   Compile a Target List of schools that interest you both academically and athletically. Consider the schools you have visited and draw on the experiences of your parents, siblings, and family friends.

☐   Meet with your guidance counselor to make sure you are taking classes to satisfy your core course requirements and to get advice on your Target List.

☐   Enroll in a prep course like Kaplan or Princeton Review to help you achieve the highest possible SAT/ACT score.

☐   Take online college surveys to help identify schools that meet your needs.

☐   Speak with your parents and family friends about their college experiences.

☐   Review your Target List of schools monthly to remove or add schools.

☐   Read college catalogs and pages of schools you are considering.

☐   Take the PSAT again.

☐   Take the SAT/ACT in the late fall/winter.

☐   Consider enrolling in AP classes.

CORRESPONDENCE

Athletics

- ❐ Register with the NCAA Clearinghouse.

- ❐ Call each college division to request a copy of their guide so you are familiar with all rules.

- ❐ Attend as many games of schools on your Target List as you can.

- ❐ Send letters of interest and your profile to coaches on your Target List, before high school starts.

- ❐ Ask your high school coach, club, summer coach or influential alumni to send letters of recommendation to schools on your Target List.

- ❐ Complete and return college questionnaires promptly.

- ❐ Seek opinions from high school coaches and other qualified persons concerning your ability to play college sports.

- ❐ Make unofficial visits to as many schools on your Target List as possible.

- ❐ Meet with the head coach of any school you visit.

- ❐ Publish your personal web site and promote it to college coaches.

- ❐ Seek national exposure by competing in national or regional competitions and showcases, and attending summer camps at your top-choice schools

- ❐ Attend a Christmas break camp if it does not conflict with your winter sport season.

- ❐ Stay in shape year round by running and lifting weights.

- ❐ Concentrate on your best position.

- ❐ Compete in a top summer leagues or for a competitive club.

Senior School Year & Summer

Academic

- ❐ Compare your GPA with your SAT/ACT score and the qualifier index.

- ❐ Retake the SAT/ACT if your scores need improvement.

- ❐ In September, request a copy of "Meeting College Costs" from your guidance office to determine how much money you need for college.

- ❐ Ask for teacher recommendations.

- ❐ Finalize your Target List and apply to these schools.

❏ Meet all application and financial aid deadlines.

❏ Evaluate your college options and consider scholarship and financial offers.

❏ Inform each college to which you've been accepted of your final decision.

❏ Fill out your FAFSA form as soon as you make your final decision

Athletics

❏ Call each college division to request a copy of their guide so you are familiar with all rules.

❏ Make unofficial and official visits to schools on your Target List.

❏ Train year round.

❏ Attend a winter camp.

❏ Increase your lifting, conditioning, and agility program.

❏ Compete at national and regional events.

❏ Contact coach at the school you get admitted to for a summer training program.

CORRESPONDENCE

The purpose of this section is to help you correspond with college coaches. Do not copy any of these letters word-for-word. Make sure you write your own versions so you stand out from the crowd. Also, many coaches are familiar with this Guide and it will look bad for you if they notice you simply retyped it.

Tips

- ◆ Type long letters but handwrite shorter ones if your writing is neat and legible. It will be more personal than if you type them (you can type your Athlete Profile).

- ◆ Individualize your letters. Do not send the same version to multiple schools. If a coach feels like you sent a bulk mailing, he will not give your letter as much attention.

- ◆ Use stationery to give your correspondence a professional appearance. You can design your own version using a nice font. Include your name, address, phone, and e-mail at the top.

- ◆ Do not call or mail letters to a college coach at his house unless he gives you permission. It's rude and you may annoy him. Always use the school address as your contact point.

- ◆ Send letters promptly. A thank-you note received the day after a meeting makes a much better impression than one received two weeks later.

Coaches evaluate the "little things" too!

Bob Temple, VarisityPages.com

Everything you do, and everything you send to a college coach, reflects on you. This includes some of the "little things" that many people may not think about.

One such little thing was a student's email address. I noticed that it referenced his favorite alcoholic beverage. When he created this email address, he probably thought it was funny. But using it was inappropriate. So, if your primary email address might give a negative impression (loudman@xyz.com or bigmanoncampus@xyz.com, for example), you might want to consider changing it, or using a different one to communicate with coaches.

Bob Temple is a sports writer who has covered all major professional sports leagues, major college sports, and high school sports throughout a 23-year writing career.

Letter of Interest
Purpose: To let a college coach know you are interested in competing for his team. Discuss your academic interests and request literature on the school and team.

Athlete Profile
Purpose: To highlight your academic and athletic accomplishments in an easy-to-read format. Include personal, athletic and academic information, references, and photo of you in your uniform. This should accompany the Letter of Interest.

Letter Accompanying a Highlight Video

Purpose: To introduce your highlight video and encourage the coach to watch it. Mention that you are sending the video because the coach asked for one. Do not send a video unless a coach requests it.

Thank You Note after a Campus Visit

Purpose: To thank a coach for taking the time to meet with you, discuss the possibility of competing for his team, and to let him know you are still interested in being recruited. Include specific examples of something pertaining to your meeting so the coach remembers you.

Letter Providing New Information

Purpose: To inform a coach of new developments and reinforce your desire to be recruited. You can send a copy of your game schedule, let the coach know that you will compete in a prestigious event, or that you just made the Dean's List.

INTERNET SITES

The web offers a wealth of college-related resources, from free test-prep courses to loan calculators to statistics on campus crime. Nevertheless, you should surf carefully. Some sites accept fees from colleges to list their schools prominently. Others require you to register and will sell your personal information to marketers if you neglect to sign complicated privacy agreements.

Moreover, when researching colleges online it's important to dig deep and think critically. Many colleges have spent thousands of dollars on fancy web sites that are little more than glitzy ads.

College Board (www.Collegeboard.com)
Collegeboard.com is one of the most comprehensive sites. It produces a customized roster of schools for students who answer questions on everything from dorms to school size. The site also contains other important information relating to the SATs and AP tests. For instance, the site lists schools that allow students with one year's worth of AP or International Baccalaureate credits to skip a year of college. In addition, it includes a free, searchable scholarship database called "LikeFinder."

US News & World Report (www.usnews.com)
Their search creates a list of potential schools based on your answers to questions about cost, geographic location, major, and several other preferences. The site features college rankings so you can identify schools according to the criteria that matter most to you, such as student-to-faculty ratio or acceptance rate. Another tool is the personality quiz. Rate the validity of 80 statements, including "I want to be able to contribute to society someday" and "friends and I enjoy discussing intellectual ideas," to find out the kinds of colleges where you'll feel at home. Need help whittling down your list? Chat with counselors and other experts on the Forum or compare the stats of up to four schools.

Once a search engine has delivered a list of possible schools, you typically can click straight to each college's home page. These pages are a popular source of information about colleges, offering course catalogs, sample financial aid packages, and virtual campus tours.

Bear in mind that much of the material on these sites is promotional. *The Internet Guide for College-Bound Students*, encourages students to browse not only the "official" pages, like the virtual tour, but to ferret out "unofficial" information as well.

Princeton Review (www.Review.com)
More hip, but more commercial, is Princeton Review's site. Its Counselor-O-Matic poses glib questions about your academic performance and interests. Then the site produces a list of colleges divided into "safety," "good match," and "reach" schools. It also has college admissions discussion boards, but you have to register to participate.

Apply On-Line
Once you have your final Target List, the Internet can make the process of applying a little easier. Many college sites have applications that either can be printed and filled out by hand or completed electronically. In addition, you can log on to one of several sites devoted to E-applications. In most cases, the services are free, although you still have to pay an application fee to the schools.

Some of them, like www.collegelink.com, www.xap.com, and www.collegenet.com, host hundreds of colleges' applications, which can be filled out and submitted electronically. You also can turn to www.commonapp.org for a generic form, called the Common Application, which is accepted by hundreds of colleges. But don't let the relative ease of applying electronically be your downfall. Too often, students who would take care with a paper form hurry through online applications. If you decide to apply online, be sure to have a parent or teacher read over your essay before you submit it.

Financial Aid (www.ed.gov/studentaid)

One of the first sites you will want to visit in your search for college funds is the Department of Education's federal student financial aid home page. The government gives grants, loans, and work-study assistance to more than 10 million students each year, and if you want to be among their ranks, you'll need to fill out their Federal Student Aid, or FAFSA. The site provides so much detailed information, however; that it can put you to sleep.

For a jazzier discussion of federal programs, check out www.finaid.org. This site also offers calculators to help you figure out how much you will get from the government and how long it will take to pay the loans back. While numerous sites provide searchable scholarship databases, stay clear of those that charge you money or "guarantee" that you'll win a scholarship; scholarship scams are prevalent.

Loans (www.wiredscholar.com)

Sallie Mae, the largest private education loan company, runs one of the best funding information sites. Easy to navigate and without registration requirements, the site has a database of hundreds of thousands of scholarships worth over a billion dollars. Why does the firm offer the site? To acquire new loan customers. In other words, if you don't find a scholarship, a private loan is just a click away.

Scholarship Database (www.fastweb.com)

With over 600,000 awards, Fastweb is one of the most aggressive in updating its scholarship database. To use the search, however, you must submit to a lengthy registration process that includes solicitations that pop up between questions. Fastweb sells registered users' names to banks and universities, and those who don't want their names released must indicate this at the beginning of the registration process.

Social Life (www.collegenews.com)

To get the skinny on the social life at a particular college, check out this site. It also has a complete listing of college newspapers.

Proofreading Application essays (www.essayedge.com)

Also worth a click is EssayEdge, a site that offers a wealth of free material on writing college essays. For a fee, their experts also will read and edit your essay.

Test Prep (www.testu.com)

TestU charges a fee for an online program based of your strengths and weaknesses. www.Number2.com takes the democratization of test prep further by offering a free interactive course.

Not to be outdone, Kaplan and Princeton Review introduced online courses, as well as free mini-courses. And even the College Board-which sponsors the SAT-has gotten in on the act with free and low-cost test prep.

Crime Reports (www.ope.ed.gov/security)

This is a good source to find out about a school's safety record. Think critically about what you read. When institutions report crime data they use different definitions of offenses so some direct comparisons among campuses may not be valid.

College Net (www.collegenet.com)
A matching service that helps you find your ideal school and on-line applications from over 1,500 colleges.

Preparing Your Child for College (www.ed.gov/studentaid)
Helps your parents with general college concerns.

Peterson's Education Center (www.petersons.com)
A leading provider of college entrance exam preparation.

College Bound Magazine (www.collegebound.net)
Informative magazine articles to help with issues facing incoming freshmen. Subscriptions available.

College Apps (www.collegeapps.com)
Collegeapps.com shows college-bound students how to personalize that very sterile college application form and market themselves to gain admission.

Collegenet (www.collegenet.com)
Provides here for your convenience over 1500 customized Internet admissions applications built for college and U. programs. When applying to more than one program you save redundant typing since common data automatically travels from form to form.

College Link (www.collegelink.com)
Assists you with your college search, applying, and making your final college decision.

Financial Aid Information Page (www.finaid.org)
Answers all questions about financial aid, loans, scholarships, and military aid.

Scholarships (www.scholarships.com)
Scholarship finder and general information about financial aid.

Financial Aid (www.fafsa.ed.gov)
An on-line version of the Free Application for Federal Student Aid

Mapping Your Future (www.mapping-your-future.org)
Helps you plan a career after college.

Career Resource Center (www.careers.org)
Assists with career advice and planning.

National Student Loan Data System (www.nslds.ed.gov)
The U.S. Department of Education's central database for student aid that receives data from schools, agencies that guarantee loans, the Direct Loan program, the Pell Grant program, and others.

INTERNET COACH ASSOCIATION SITES

Soccer:

National Soccer Coaches Association of America (www.nscaa.com)
Founded in 1941, the NSCAA is the largest coaches' organization in the US. The organization provides an extensive awards program for over 10,000 individuals and also provides national rankings for high school and colleges.

Field Hockey:

National Field Hockey Coaches Association (www.eteamz.com/NFHCA)
Provides a recognizable presence and voice in regard to legislation affecting the sport of Field Hockey as well as interscholastic and intercollegiate programs

Intercollegiate Women's Lacrosse Coaches Association (www.iwlca.org)
The IWLCA is the peak national body for women's lacrosse in the United States. Its mission is to foster and develop the sport nationwide.

Lacrosse:

United States Intercollegiate Lacrosse Association (www.usila.org)
Sponsors rankings of the top collegiate teams and provides information and news on the latest developments in college lacrosse.

Track:

American Track Coaches Association (www.abca.org)
Features instructional articles, national poll results, and interesting feature stories.

National Collegiate Athletic Association (www.ncaa.org)
Represents 1,024 four-year schools in three separate divisions (I, II, and III).

National Association of Intercollegiate Athletics (http://www.naia.org)
Represents 180 four-year schools.

National Junior College Athletic Association (www.njcaa.org)
Represents 503 two-year programs representing three separate divisions (I, II, and III).

Volleyball:

American Volleyball Coaches Assistant (www.avca.org)
Although most services focus on volleyball coaches, the organization's website has a comprehensive listing of camps available for searching.

Water Polo:

USA Water Polo (www.usawaterpolo.com)
Provides valuable content on current collegiate programs and athletes and upcoming tournaments and championships.

Basketball:

Women's Basketball Coaches Association (www.wbca.org)
Provides information on collegiate programs as well as coaches. In addition, the organization sponsors an "All-

Star" game for talented high school seniors and provides listings of camps and clinics.
National Association of Basketball Coaches (www.nabc.org)
Provides comprehensive news about men's college basketball, including useful links that update the latest developments in recruiting trends.

Fencing:
United States Fencing (www.usfencing.org)
Provides information about individual tournaments and competitions as well as a national ranking scheme.

Hockey:
American Hockey Coaches Association (www.ahca.org)
Provides information on awards programs for collegiate athletes and has bibliographic information on a variety of college coaches.

Swimming:
College Swimming Coaches Of America Association (www.cscaa.org)
Gives access to top collegiate swimming times, teams, coaches, and athletes in the NCAA Divisions I, II, III and the NAIA.

Golf:
College Golf Foundation (www.cgfgolf.org)
Provides a rating scheme for collegiate programs and organizes college tournaments as well as providing a comprehensive list of links dealing with collegiate golf.

Tennis:
College Tennis Online (www.collegetennisonline.com)
Primarily filled with news content and scores, this site also provides links to college camps, collegiate teams and program rankings.

COLLEGE INFORMATION SHEET

The best way to keep your college materials organized is to print this sheet for each school on your Target List. Place each sheet—along with any school catalogs or other information you receive—inside a file folder. Write the school's name on the outside of the folder.

General

School_____ Division:_____

Address_____City_____State_____Zip____

Admissions Dept Phone_____Web Page_____

Academics

Academic Rating: ❏ Most Competitive ❏ Average ❏ Less Competitive ❏ Not Competitive

Potential Major/Departments of interest_____

Prestige of degree: ❏ Very Prestigious   ❏ Average ❏ Not Prestigious

Undergraduate Enrollment_____Faculty:Student Ratio_____

Average GPA of accepted applicants_____Average SAT/ACT scores_____

Likelihood of being accepted: ❏ Safety School ❏ Likely ❏ Reach

Conversation notes with admission department (include date & what you discussed)

_____

_____

Athletics

Head Coach_____Recruiting Coordinator_____

Assistant Coach(es)_____

Athletic Office Phone_____E-mail addresses_____

Coach's interest: ❏ Recruiting me heavily ❏ Slight interest ❏ No discussions yet ❏ None

Athletes in my sport_____How many recruited at my position_____

Likelihood of contributing: ❏ Definitely ❏ Maybe ❏ Slim Chance

Been to a game?_____ Compete on TV? _____

Does coach want me to red-shirt?   ❒ Yes ❒ No Graduation rate of athletes:_____

Scholarship offered?   ❒ No ❒ Yes Amount_____

Competitive schedule?   ❒ Yes ❒ No   Overnight trips: ❒ Yes ❒ No

Offered an Official Visit: ❒ No ❒ Yes When_____

Unofficial Visit planned?   ❒ No ❒ Yes When_____

Athletic Facilities (fields, weight room):   ❒ Excellent   ❒ Average   ❒ Poor

Strength of team/schedule: ❒ Excellent   ❒ Average   ❒ Weak

Conversation notes with coaches (include date & what you discussed)

_____

_____

Finances

Tuition_____ Room & Board_____ Transportation To/From Home _____

How much of a financial aid/ scholarship package do I need to afford this school?_____

Conversation notes with financial aid department (include date & what you discussed): _____

_____

_____

Other Considerations

Housing: ❒ On-campus dorm ❒ Off-campus apartment

Campus Life: ❒ Lots of activities ❒ Average   ❒ Little to do

Greek Life: ❒ Big ❒ Average ❒ Small   ❒ None

Transportation home: ❒ Fly   Duration of trip_____ ❒ Drive   Duration of trip_____

Friends, relatives, or high school alumni who have gone to this school:_____

Would I be happy at this school if I didn't play sports? ❒ Yes ❒ No

IDENTIFY YOUR #1 SCHOOL

If you have trouble selecting a school that you want to attend, complete this exercise after you receive your acceptance letters.

1. Specify how important each of the following criteria is to you by checking in one of the three boxes I abeled "Very," "Somewhat" or "Not." This will help focus your decision.
2. Rank what you feel is "Very Important" to you on a scale of 1-5 (5 being best).
3. Add up all the rankings. If this doesn't clearly identify your #1 choice, then you can rank all the criteria that you feel are "Somewhat Important."

IMPORTANCE TO ME?			CRITERIA	SCHOOL #1 ( )	SCHOOL #2 ( )	SCHOOL #3 ( )
Very	Somewhat	Not				
			Academics			
☐	☐	☐	School's reputation	_____	_____	_____
☐	☐	☐	Fields of study	_____	_____	_____
☐	☐	☐	Prestige of degree	_____	_____	_____
☐	☐	☐	Professors	_____	_____	_____
☐	☐	☐	Class size	_____	_____	_____
☐	☐	☐	Alumni network	_____	_____	_____
☐	☐	☐	Small enrollment	_____	_____	_____
☐	☐	☐	In-State	_____	_____	_____
☐	☐	☐	Out-of-State	_____	_____	_____
☐	☐	☐	Athletic Tutoring	_____	_____	_____
			Athletics			
☐	☐	☐	Scholarships	_____	_____	_____
☐	☐	☐	Chance to Play	_____	_____	_____
☐	☐	☐	High-profile team/conf	_____	_____	_____
☐	☐	☐	Transfer opportunities	_____	_____	_____
☐	☐	☐	Caliber of team	_____	_____	_____
☐	☐	☐	Competitive schedule	_____	_____	_____
☐	☐	☐	Coaching staff	_____	_____	_____
☐	☐	☐	Athletic facilities	_____	_____	_____
☐	☐	☐	Graduation rate	_____	_____	_____
			Other			
☐	☐	☐	My parents approve	_____	_____	_____
☐	☐	☐	Location	_____	_____	_____
☐	☐	☐	Climate	_____	_____	_____
☐	☐	☐	Greek life	_____	_____	_____
☐	☐	☐	Distance from home	_____	_____	_____
☐	☐	☐	Campus events	_____	_____	_____
☐	☐	☐	Social life	_____	_____	_____
☐	☐	☐	Meet new people	_____	_____	_____
☐	☐	☐	Out-of-pocket cost	_____	_____	_____
			Grand Total	_____	_____	_____

COST OF COLLEGE COMPARISON

EXPENSES	SCHOOL #1	SCHOOL #2	SCHOOL #3
	(_____)	(_____)	(_____)
Tuition & Fees	_____	_____	_____
Room & Board	_____	_____	_____
Books & Supplies	_____	_____	_____
Personal Expenses	_____	_____	_____
Transportation	_____	_____	_____
Other	_____	_____	_____
TOTAL EXPENSES	_____	_____	_____
TOTAL FINANCIAL AID	_____	_____	_____
YOUR ANNUAL COST	_____	_____	_____

(Total Expenses minus Total Financial Aid)

ESTIMATED FAMILY CONTRIBUTION

This chart provides an approximation of how much financial aid departments will expect your family to contribute toward your college expenses each year.

The figures are based on only one parent working, no other siblings in college, and no unusual financial circumstances. You should also add a $700-$1,000 student contribution to the final amount. These figures are only estimates. Your actual contribution may vary.

2005-2006 Estimated Parent Contribution

Net Assets of $25,000

Family Size / Income Before Taxes	3	4	5	6
$20,000	$0	$0	$0	$0
$30,000	$1,060	$230	$0	$0
$40,000	$2,690	$1,900	$1,160	$290
$50,000	$4,680	$3,600	$2,750	$1,910
$60,000	$7,550	$5,990	$4,780	$3,620
$70,000	$10,950	$9,260	$7,680	$6,020
$80,000	$14,210	$12,660	$11,080	$9,290

Net Assets of $50,000

Family Size / Income Before Taxes	3	4	5	6
$20,000	$0	$0	$0	$0
$30,000	$1,380	$560	$0	$0
$40,000	$3,050	$2,220	$1,480	$610
$50,000	$5,180	$4,030	$3,120	$2,230
$60,000	$8,240	$6,580	$5,280	$4,050
$70,000	$11,640	$9,950	$8,370	$6,610
$80,000	$14,910	$13,350	$11,770	$9,990

Net Assets of $100,000

Family Size / Income Before Taxes	3	4	5	6
$20,000	$1,000	$130	$0	$0
$30,000	$2,700	$1,880	$1,100	$230
$40,000	$4,760	$3,670	$2,810	$1,930
$50,000	$7,660	$6,090	$4,860	$3,690
$60,000	$11,060	$9,370	$7,790	$6,120
$70,000	$14,460	$12,770	$11,190	$9,400
$80,000	$16,560	$16,170	$14,590	$12,810

Please note that the charts assume the following:

* Two parents in the family, both employed and earning equal wages.
* Income only from employment.
* The family has no unusual financial circumstances, such as high medical expenses.
* The standard deduction is used when calculating taxes on the 1040 form.
* One child is enrolled in college when college expenses must be paid.
* Calculations are according to the "federal methodology," which is used to determine federal aid, and which some schools follow (VSAC uses a slightly different methodology for determining Vermont grants); the federal methodology excludes the value of a family's home or farm.
* Calculations are based on 2004 income and apply to the 2005-2006 academic year.

FINISH LINE: Different people can use the forms and checklists in this section at different stages of the process. Begin with the checklists at the beginning of the chapter. Even if you're a junior already, go back through the freshman and sophomore checklists and determine if you completed all the items. Then bring yourself up to date to your current class.

Begin working on your correspondence. Check out some of the Web sites listed, and use the other forms as appropriate.

GLOSSARY OF TERMS

ACT A curriculum-based college admissions test. The multiple choice questions that test English, Mathematics, Reading, and Science Reasoning on the ACT are a measure of what you've learned in your high school classes rather than aptitude or IQ. Most U.S. colleges accept ACT results.

Advanced Placement Courses (AP) High school courses that can result in college credit, depending on your final exam score. College admissions officers generally look upon AP courses favorably as evidence of a challenging high school program.

Amateurism To be eligible to play college sports, students must maintain their amateur status.

Athletic Scholarship A form of financial aid that can be used to pay for tuition and fees, room and board, and books. It can be guaranteed for only one year at a time and must be renewed each year. Many coaches will verbally commit to and honor a four- or five-year scholarship even though they cannot put it in writing.

Award Letter A statement sent to you by colleges that have accepted you which recaps the amount and type of aid the college can offer.

Blue-Chip Recruit A highly sought-after high school athlete who attracts the attention of a wide variety of high-profile college coaches and pro scouts. This gifted athlete possesses outstanding athletic ability, a tremendous work ethic, and generally excellent academic marks.

Booster This person is usually a wealthy alumnus of the school with close ties to the athletic department. You will be ineligible for college athletics if you have any recruiting contact with boosters or alumni not employed by the college.

Bylaw 14.3 NCAA D-I and D-II legislation that requires you to meet a minimum GPA, SAT/ACT scores, take certain core courses, and graduate from high school before you can play college sports.

California Community Colleges Or CCC A small college division featuring 14 junior colleges in California. These schools do not offer scholarships.

Clearinghouse The organization responsible for certifying the academic eligibility for practice, competition and financial aid of all prospective student-athletes for Division I and Division II.

College Board A not-for-profit organization that administers many standardized tests including the PSAT, SAT, SAT II, and AP. Additionally, the College Board offers official test prep materials, a scholarship search, a personal inventory tool, and educational loans.

Commercial Loans or Private/Alternative Loans Commercial loans are available through several financial services providers. To qualify, you must pass a credit check, and the interest rate will be higher than that of a Direct or FFEL Stafford or Perkins Loan. For these reasons, it is wise to investigate low-interest, federally-sponsored options before applying for a commercial loan. In addition, beware of scholarship scams that are simply commercial loans in disguise.

Community College See Junior College

Contacts Any face-to-face meeting in excess of a greeting between you and a college coach or member of the athletic department. You may only be contacted off campus after July 1 before your senior year. Coaches may not contact you off campus more than three times.

Contact Period During this time, a college coach may have in-person contact with a student and/or the student's parents on or off the college's campus. The coach may also watch a student play or visit the student's high school. Students may visit the college campus and coaches may write or telephone students during this period.

Co-op An education that integrates classroom study with paid, supervised work experiences. These jobs are part or full-time and may lead to academic credit.

Core Courses Specified college preparatory courses that you need to take while in high school in order to be an eligible NCAA recruit.

Dead Period A period of time when a college coach may not have any in-person contact with a student or his or her family. The coach may write or call the student or the student's parents during this time.

Direct Expenses The total cost of tuition and fees, room and board, and books.

Early Signing Period One week in mid-November during which you can sign a National Letter of Intent.

Expected Family Contribution (EFC) The total you are expected to contribute toward the cost of college. The federal government determines the amount of your EFC based on the information you supply on the FAFSA and the total cost of attendance for the college of your choice. The total cost includes tuition, room and board, books, transportation, and other personal expenses. You will fill out the FAFSA each year, which may alter the EFC for each year of college.

Electronic Application An alternative to traditional paper applications, electronic applications can take several forms. Some schools allow you to print application forms from their Web site or a CD-ROM, which you can fill in by hand and mail to the admissions office. Other schools support online applications that you can fill out and submit over the web. If you decide to apply electronically, you will not have to wait to receive materials in the mail. Best of all, applying electronically will get your application in the hands of admissions officers sooner.

Evaluations Any off-campus activity used to assess your athletic ability. A coach may evaluate you at your high school or any other venue. NCAA D-III schools are not permitted to arrange an evaluation of you.

Financial Aid Package Each college has its own custom package, which may include federal and state grants, independent sources, school scholarships, student loans, and on-campus jobs. This provides you with a comparison guide among schools on your Target List.

Free Application For Federal Student Aid (FAFSA) The FAFSA is used to apply for federal student financial aid, including grants, loans, and work-study. In addition, it is used by most schools to award non-federal student financial aid. The form is a summary of your family's financial situation including income, debt, and assets for both you and your parents. You will have to fill out the FAFSA every year that you are in college.

Family Contribution The amount of money your family is expected to pay toward the Student Expense Budget. This amount is a fixed sum determined by the Federal Methodology and it will be the same regardless of what school you apply to.

Fellowships Available to students in most disciplines and sponsored by colleges and a broad range of organizations and institutions. Fellowships offered by organizations are often allocated in monthly stipends and can usually be used at any university. Fellowships are more common at the graduate level, but some undergraduate scholarships do exist. Additionally, there may be grant and fellowship money available for specific research projects or study abroad. Contact your major department, financial aid office, or career center for more information.

Federal Family Education Loan Program (FFEL) Low-interest education loans made by private lenders to students and parents. These loans may be either subsidized or unsubsidized, and there are several repayment plans available.

Financial Aid Any type of assistance used to help you meet college costs. It is divided into two categories: Gift Aid (athletic and academic scholarships and grants), and Self-Help Aid (loans and work study).

Federal Supplemental Educational Opportunity Grants (FSEOG) Government-sponsored, college-administered loans awarded to exceptionally needy students. Eligibility is determined by the federal government and the program gives priority to students receiving federal support.

Full Athletic Scholarship Or Full Ride Terms used when the college pays 100% of the expenses. These are rare and are usually given only to "blue-chip" athletes.

General Educational Development Test (GED) The GED may take the place of high-school graduation under certain conditions. If a student has the GED, he or she must still have the required number of core courses, the required grade-point average and the required ACT or SAT score.

Grant Aid This is the most sought-after type of financial aid because it does not have to be paid back. You may receive grant aid on the basis of either need or merit, and it may come from your school or the federal government. Federal grants include the need-based Pell and Federal Supplemental Educational Opportunity (FSEOG) grants.

Grayshirt A student who is recruited out of high school, but who delays full-time enrollment in college for a term or terms

Good Academic Standing Maintaining at least a C average while in college.

Home School A student who does not attend a traditional high school. A student who has been educated at home must register with the clearing-house like any other student.

Hook When you write your admissions essays, you'll want to engage your readers quickly. Using your "hook," a unique personal trait or experience, is one way to achieve this goal. If you are a dedicated and accomplished cellist or have trekked through the Himalayas, these might make good starting points for college essays. Your hook will be something about you that is unique and interesting.

Hope Credit A nonrefundable federal income tax credit equal to all of the first $1,000 out-of-pocket payments for qualified tuition and related expenses and 50% of the second $1,000, for a maximum $1,500 per student, per year. The Hope credit applies to the first two years of post-secondary education. You may not claim both the Hope Credit and the Lifetime Learning Credit (see below).
Indirect Expenses The total cost of transportation to and from school, incidental expenses, and supplies.

Ivy League The athletic conference that boasts academic powerhouses Brown, Columbia, Cornell, Dartmouth, Harvard, Penn, Princeton, and Yale. Acceptance to an Ivy League school is considered the brass ring of the application process, although many argue that an equal, if not better, education can be achieved at many non-Ivy League schools.

Junior College Or JC Or Juco Represents all two-year schools including community colleges. These schools provide college courses for recent high school graduates and adults in their communities. JCs generally have fewer admissions requirements than four-year institutions and courses typically cost less than comparable courses at four-year schools. Many students use JC as a springboard to a four-year college or U..

Lab Sciences High school science courses which supplement textbook study with hands-on experimentation. Examples include biology, chemistry, and physics. Other courses, such as economics, may be considered scientific disciplines, but do not qualify as lab sciences. Consult your guidance counselor or your prospective college's admissions office for further details.

Late Signing Period One week in mid-April during which you can sign a National Letter of Intent.

Letter Of Intent Or LOI A four-page contract, administered by the Collegiate Commissioners Association, that commits you to attend a specific college. If you change your mind after signing the letter, you must be mutually released from your commitment by the old school and your new school. In addition, you cannot play for one year and you lose a year of eligibility. This is a serious contract that should not be taken lightly.

Lifetime Learning Credit The Lifetime Learning Credit may be claimed for your tuition and related expenses on your parents' tax returns. Through 2002, the amount that may be claimed as a credit is equal to 20% of the taxpayer's first $5,000 of out-of-pocket qualified tuition and related expenses for all the students in the family for a maximum of $1,000. Individuals with modified adjusted gross incomes of $50,000 or more and joint filers with modified adjusted gross incomes of $100,000 or more are not eligible for the Lifetime Learning Credit.

Likely Letter A letter sent to an athletic scholarship recipient in the fall or early winter that lets him know the likelihood of being accepted to the school and the probable size of the financial package he will receive.

Merit-Based Aid Or Merit Scholarships Any form of financial aid not based on demonstrated financial need. Each school and/or its alumni associations and wealthy benefactors generally grant merit-based aid, which can take the form of grants, athletic or academic scholarships, or loans on favorable terms. You may qualify for it by meeting a certain academic requirement, such as GPA, test scores, a career goal, or through an essay competition. Your financial aid package may include both Need and Merit-based aid.

National Association of Intercollegiate Athletics (NAIA) The NAIA represents smaller schools and can provide scholarships.

National Merit Scholarship A distinction award you can receive if you score high enough on the NMSQT/PSAT (National Merit Scholar Qualifying Test/Preliminary Scholastic Aptitude Test). The test may be administered for practice during your sophomore year, but only your junior-year score counts.

National Collegiate Athletic Association (NCAA) The main association for intercollegiate athletics, the NCAA is made up of three divisions—I, II, and III. Division I and II offer track scholarships.

National Junior College Athletic Association (NJCAA) The association that overseas two-year programs. The NJCAA is divided into three divisions—I, II, and III. Divisions I and II offer track scholarships. See also Junior college.

NCAA Clearinghouse An organization established by the NCAA that determines if you are eligible for an official visit and to be recruited by NCAA D-I or D-II schools. You should register with the Clearinghouse at the start of your junior year of high school.

Need-Based Aid If the cost of attendance for your college exceeds your Expected Family Contribution (EFC), you will be eligible for need-based aid to cover the difference. You may be awarded a financial-aid package that consists of a combination of grants, scholarships, loans, and work-study. The total amount of your package will be determined by a combination of demonstrated financial need, federal award maximums, and your school's available funds.

Nonqualifier A nonqualifier cannot practice, compete or receive institutional financial aid for one academic year in Division I and II, and has three seasons of competition in Division I.

Official Visit Your trip to a college campus, paid in whole or in part by that institution. You are permitted by the NCAA to take one expense-paid visit to each of five different schools that are recruiting you during your senior year, regardless of how many sports you play. Visits are limited to 48 hours. You must pay for all additional visits.

Partial Qualifier You can receive a scholarship, practice, but not play games during your first year of school. If you are able to complete your academic degree in four years, you may stay at school a fifth year, giving you four years of eligibility.

Patriot League The NCAA D-I athletic conference that includes Bucknell, U.S. Military Academy, Lehigh, U.S. Naval Academy, American U., Lafayette, and Holy Cross, and does not offer track scholarships except for American.

Pell Grants Given by the Federal Government, these grants are awarded to those students demonstrating exceptional financial need. Pell grants do not need to be paid back.

Perkins Loans Awarded by each school, these low-interest loans (around 5%) are given to students who demonstrate exceptional financial need. Repayment of this loan begins nine months after you graduate, leave school, or drop to less than half-time student status.

Perkins & Stafford Loan Two types of need-based loans that are regularly included within a student's need-based financial aid package.

Personal Identification Number (PIN) When a student registers with the clearinghouse, he or she picks a four-digit PIN. This PIN will allow the student to check his or her eligibility online or by phone. For high schools, each school selects a five-digit PIN that allows high-school personnel to access specific information through the clearinghouse Web site.

The Parent Loans For Undergraduate Students (PLUS) And Supplemental Loans For Students (SLS) Two federal programs that assist families who don't qualify for need-based aid or who need help with their family contribution.

Private Counselors You may consult private counselors as you prepare to select and apply to colleges. They may operate as consultants or as employees of educational service providers such as Kaplan or the Princeton Review. Private counselors can help you assess your personality and academic needs to form a list of desirable college attributes. They can also help you figure out where and to how many schools you should apply. Private counselors can give you more attention than the average high school guidance counselor, but they can be pricey.

Profile The CSS/Financial Aid PROFILE is a customized financial aid application form required at certain colleges, which collects additional financial information to determine eligibility for institutional aid.

Proposition 48 This law states that a student athlete must meet certain requirements if he wants to practice and play during his freshman year at a NCAA Division I or Division II school.

Prospective Student Athlete Once you begin your freshmen year of high school, you may meet with college coaches but only if you initiate contact during an unofficial visit.

Preliminary Standard Aptitude Test (PSAT) The PSAT is administered by the college Board. You may take the PSAT in order to familiarize yourself with the test and kinds of questions you'll encounter on the SAT. The PSAT is also used as the qualifying test for the National Merit Scholar competition. This test is usually taken during your junior year of high school, but a practice PSAT may be given during your sophomore year. Like the SAT, the PSAT uses multiple-choice questions to test verbal and mathematical reasoning ability.

Qualifier A qualifier may practice, compete and receive institutional financial aid in his or her first year of enrollment at a Division I or II college.

Quiet period The college coach may not have any in-person contact with a student or the student's parents off the college campus. The coach may not watch the student play or visit the student's high school during this time. The student and his or her parents may visit a college campus during this time. A coach may write or telephone a student or his or her parents during this time.

Redshirt A term that describes you if you sit out a year of competition. If you are injured during your freshmen year or your college coach feels you need an extra year to develop, he may "redshirt" you. You would be permitted to practice with the team but not allowed to play in games. Redshirt athletes must complete their four years of athletic eligibility within six years.

SAT II The SAT II assesses knowledge in various subject areas. Most colleges require the writing test, a math test, and a foreign language test. They are taken in the spring of your junior year and the fall of your senior year. If the test is linked to a specific subject like chemistry, it's best to take the test as soon as possible upon the completion of the course.

© 2009 Mazz Marketing, Inc. | 203 260 4932 | wayne@waynemazzoni.com | WayneMazzoni.com

Scholarship A type of financial aid that does not require repayment or employment and is usually awarded to students who demonstrate potential for academic or athletic achievement.

Scholastic Assessment Test (SAT) The SAT is administered by the College Board and is the most widely used college admissions test. The SAT uses multiple-choice questions to assess verbal and mathematical reasoning ability and an essay section. The SAT is taken during your junior and/or senior years. You may take this test multiple times if you wish to improve your score.

Sliding Scale A provision of the NCAA's Bylaw 14.3 that calculates minimum GPA and SAT/ACT scores in order for you to be an eligible recruit. The higher your GPA, the lower your SAT/ACT requirement, and visa-versa.

Sports Agent Someone who wants to handle all of your affairs (contract negotiation, sponsorships, financial planning, etc) should you make it to the pros. You are in violation of NCAA rules if you agree to let a sports agent represent you while you are still in high school or college.

Student-Expense Budget The total cost of attending a certain college for one academic year. Your financial need determined by the federal need analysis formula is the difference between the total cost of attending a college and your Family's Expected Contribution.

Student Release Form A document that you and your guidance counselor complete verifying your academic eligibility to compete at a NCAA D-I or D-II school.

Stafford Loans These loans, both subsidized (need based) and unsubsidized (non-need based), are guaranteed by the federal government and available to fund your education. Federal Stafford Loans are the most common source of education loan funds.

Student Aid Report (SAR) The official notification sent to you four to six weeks after filing the FAFSA. This report explains your FEC in relation to your school's expected cost of attendance. You may be required to submit this document to the financial aid office at the college you decide to attend.

Subsidized Loans Subsidized loans are based upon financial need. With these loans, the interest is paid by the federal government until the repayment period begins and during authorized periods of deferment afterwards.

Test Prep Preparing you for the college admissions tests is big business. There are books, videos, CD-ROMs, and classroom courses you can purchase designed to help you do your best on the tests. It is wise to do some prep for the test. At a minimum, look over the informational packet about each test to familiarize yourself with the number and type of questions you'll be expected to answer. And don't expect miracles—you'll have to do some hard work to make any kind of test prep successful.

Title IX Also referred to as gender equity, this law mandates that institutions that receive federal funding, among other things, are not allowed to discriminate on the basis of sex. This means that schools have had to increase funding and opportunities for women's athletics.

Transcript Your high school academic record. Your guidance counselor or registrar compiles this list of all your courses, grades, and standardized test scores. Your college will ask for official copies of your transcript. They should be signed across the seal by the appropriate school official and should not be opened.

Transfer Despite your best efforts, you may find that your chosen school isn't the perfect fit, or, you may start out at junior college and decide that it's time to attend a four-year University. In either case, you may need to transfer to a different school. Transferring can be a tricky process, especially when it comes time to figure out how many of your previously earned credits will count at your new school. To make your transition as simple as possible, request application materials from prospective schools as early as possible and figure out how your credits will be accounted for before you apply.

University Universities generally support both undergraduate and graduate programs and tend to be larger than colleges. You may find more research opportunities at a U., but you might get less attention from professors than at a college.

Unofficial Visit Any visit to a college campus by a student or his or her parents, paid for by the student or the student's parents. The only expense a student may receive is three complimentary admissions to a home contest.

Unsubsidized Loans Unsubsidized loans are not need-based; so all students are eligible to receive them. Interest payments begin immediately on unsubsidized loans, although you can waive the payments and the interest will be capitalized.

Verbal Commitment When a student verbally indicates that, he or she plans to attend a college or university and play college sports there. A verbal commitment is not binding for the college or the student.

Waiver A process to set aside NCAA rules because of specific, extraordinary circumstances that prevented a student from meeting the rules. A college on behalf of the student must file a waiver.

Walk-ons Usually unrecruited athletes who make the roster by proving themselves at open tryouts. This is difficult depending on the school. Some schools rely on walk ons to fill out their team while others discourage walk-ons. Make sure you would be comfortable attending the school if you do not end up competing for the team.

Weighted GPA Some high schools add 0.5 grade points to grades earned in AP or IB courses to reflect their unusual level of difficulty. If you have taken such courses, your GPA may be considered weighted. Some colleges convert weighted GPAs to standard GPAs for the purposes of comparison.

Work-study An institutionally or federally funded employment program that provides students with part-time jobs—generally 10 to 15 hours per week.

COLLEGIATE ATHLETICS IN CANADA

If you are thinking of competing at the collegiate level in Canada, there are a few things you should know. In Canada, the Canadian Inter-University Athletic Union (CIAU) is the equivalent of the NCAA. Regional champions from each of the five CIAU conferences compete at the CIAU National Championships each year.

In any given year, over 10,000 student athletes compete in 3,000 events scheduled from September to March. The CIAU National Championships features athletes in the following sports: soccer, cross country, indoor track and field, field hockey, football, basketball, ice hockey, wrestling, swimming, and volleyball.

History of CAIU

Founded in 1906, the original existed until 1955. Then it was only composed of universities in Ontario and Quebec. By 1955, the CIAU expanded to include nineteen universities in other provinces. Before total integration, individual provinces devised their own, unique athletic associations, following their own set of rules. Finally, in the 1970's the CIAU was formed as a universal association for all of Canada.

Can A U.S. Resident Attend School In Canada?

Yes, however, admission rules vary for foreign students. Canadian universities do offer student-athlete financial assistance. The financial aid is not on the same scale as the United States, but it is cheaper to attend college in Canada.

Before a student is given financial aid from a school, it has to be approved by the CIAU. Each year more than 300 awards are offered to varsity athletes by universities across the country to assist in covering the cost of tuition. The amount of money varies; however, the award may not exceed a maximum amount of $1,500(Canadian dollars).

Canadians usually go to college in Canada, but there are some student athletes who do come to U.S. schools and play sports on scholarship. However, there is no such thing as a "full ride" at a Canadian school. So, if you're a U.S. student athlete, and you want to go to a Canadian school, call the coach before you make any financially based decisions. For more information about the CIAU, visit www.ciau.ca.

INTERNATIONAL STUDENTS

If you are an international student considering playing sports at an American college or university, you are not alone. Thousands of international students pursue a college athletic experience each year within the United States.

If you are not a U.S. citizen and you are interested in competing at the college level in the United States, then here is what you will need to do:

- With thousands of college programs to choose from, you will need to get help from a good advisor.

- If English is not your first language, you will need to take the Test of English as a Foreign Language (TOEFL) or provide evidence that your are proficient in English. Most colleges and universities differ on the score needed for acceptance into the school, but usually a score of 213 is suitable for the most prestigious schools in America.

- You may also need to take the SAT or ACT. Most colleges and universities ask to see both the SAT and TOEFL results of international student athletes.

- You should begin both the recruitment and application process more than a year in advance. The earlier you start talking with coaches and admissions officers the better your chances are of getting admitted and competing at the school of your choice.

- You will need to obtain an I-20 Certificate of Eligibility from the school you plan to attend and also an F-1.

10 THINGS TO REMEMBER DURING THE RECRUITING PROCESS

Though there are many ways to attract a college coach's attention, if you make use of the following ten suggestions, you will be ahead of your competition:

1. **Succeed In The Classroom.** You must achieve certain academic requirements to be eligible to play college sports. Don't let poor grades limit your choices. Strive for excellence!

2. **Keep An Open Mind.** Even if you have your heart set on one college team, keep your options open with a wide range of schools on your Target List.

3. **Promote Yourself To College Coaches.** Don't wait for coaches to find you. Call, write, or email coaches to let them know that you want to play for their team.

4. **Use All Your Resources.** Get your parents, high school coach, summer league coach, and guidance counselor involved in the recruiting process.

5. **Improve Your Entire Package.** A good attitude, character, work ethic, and hustle are all important attributes that college coaches look for in athletes.

6. **Attend Showcases, Tournaments And Prospect Camps.** These events are perfect opportunities to demonstrate your ability to many college coaches and pro scouts. They also let you see how you stack up with other athletes in your area.

7. **Explore All Sources Of Financial Aid.** Many students receive other sources of financial aid, not just athletic scholarships.

8. **Learn About All Your Options.** Become familiar with the different divisions and keep an open mind. Visit different campuses, use the Internet to research college websites, and ask questions. Remember, you are not only choosing a place to compete athletically, but you are selecting a new home.

9. **Set Goals And Deadlines.** Make lists of academic and athletic accomplishments that you want to achieve during each year of high school.

10. **Have Fun.** Play for the love of the game.

HOW DID WE DO?

Thank you for purchasing *GET RECRUITED: The Definitive Guide to Playing College Sports.* Even though we are confident of our ability to help athletes like you navigate the recruiting process, we are always striving to improve. We would appreciate your input on what we can do to make this Guide more educational for future readers.

Your name (optional): _____

Your email address: _____

	Very	A Lot	Somewhat	Not Really	Not at all
How relevant was the Guide's information?	☐	☐	☐	☐	☐
How thorough was the Guide?	☐	☐	☐	☐	☐
How accurate was the Guide's information?	☐	☐	☐	☐	☐
How easy was the Guide to use?	☐	☐	☐	☐	☐
How appealing was the Guide's design?	☐	☐	☐	☐	☐

What overall grade would you give the Guide? (1-10, 10 being the best) _____

What were the Guide's strongest points?_____

How could the Guide be improved? _____

Was there anything not in the Guide that you wanted to know more about?_____

Would you recommend this book to other athletes?   ☐ Yes   ☐ No

Other Comments: _____

_____

May we use your comments for promotional purposes?   ☐ Yes   ☐ No

Thank you for your help!

Please tear out this page and mail it to:

Mazz Marketing, Inc.
287 Courtland Avenue
Black Rock, CT 06605

© 2009 Mazz Marketing, Inc. | 203 260 4932 | wayne@waynemazzoni.com | WayneMazzoni.com